EVEN MORE MUCK

More Humorous Farming Tales
From
Joyce Wilson

Best Wishes

Joyce Wilson

Published by Seatallan Press
6 Downfield Lane, Bigrigg, Egremont,
Cumbria CA22 2UY

First published 1997
Reprinted 1999

Typeset in 10/12pt Meridian by
Deltatype Ltd, Birkenhead, Merseyside.
Printed and bound in Great Britain by
Athenaeum Press Ltd, Newcastle upon Tyne

British Library Cataloguing in Publication Data
A catalogue record for this book is available
from the British Library

ISBN 0 9528919 0 5

CONTENTS

To my son Paul and his wife Janice

1

FINDING A CURE

'**G**ood God! What's the matter with you this morning Tom?' exclaimed Jackson as his friend leant heavily against the byre door jamb.

'I feel bloody awful . . .'

'It's not like you to feel bad on any day except Sunday morning. Has that wicked friesian you were daft enough to buy the other week kicked the hell out of you?'

'It feels like it Jackson, but our farm lad had to do all the milking by himself this morning . . . it took me a good hour to get crawled out of bed and down to breakfast. It's me rheumatics! I'm crippled to bits today.'

'What made you struggle over to see me then. You'd be much better stopping in bed for half a day. Leave the work for the rest of them to do . . . it does the family the world of good to take over for a day or two. It lets them see how hard you have to work *every* day. There's no need to make a martyr of yourself . . . you wouldn't catch me dragging myself about like a dying fox.'

'Mary tried to get me to drive in to Egremont to see the doctor, but I remember you once said that you had some sort of lotion that you rubbed on your back when you weren't so good. Maybe you'd give me what's left. I don't have time to sit about in the doctor's surgery all morning.'

'A spot I've never been to. But whenever any of the womenfolk have to go it's a day's work . . . and they're jiggered when they get back. I reckon if you're fit enough to walk all the way in to Egremont to see a doctor, then there's nowt much wrong with you in the first place.'

Tom did his best to nod in assent, but the effort made him pull a face with the pain.

'I suppose I could ask him to call round.'

Jackson shook his head in vigorous disapproval.

'The whole area would think you were at death's door. You know how gossip travels ... us farmers are usually desperate if we call either a doctor or a vet to the house. Everybody knows that we manage as best we can without resorting to unnecessary expense. Once them chaps get you in their clutches, your hands are never out of your pocket ... aye, a dear do before we can get anything decently buried.'

'You talk as though they never heal anybody Jackson, but I wouldn't like to rely on the old wives' remedies we had years ago ... I remember the pain of a bad toothache, them remedies didn't seem to do any good, but that dentist in Egremont can pull out a bad tooth before you know he's got his hands in your mouth.'

'That's not what they tell me ... they reckon you have to be in bad pain to have the courage to walk through his door. A good many folks would rather stick the agony ... in any case the pain goes eventually and the tooth crumbles away to leave a strong pair of gums. Mine'll eat owt ... vanity Tom ... vanity ... that's what makes folk, especially women, visit a dentist. You know Tom, women can stand the sort of pain that would put the likes of you and me ... or any strong man, into our beds on our back for a week. Don't let any of them tell you that they're the weakest sex! It just isn't bloody-well true.'

'Come on now Jackson. Don't you think you're a bit hard on the women?'

'No chap would think of strapping himself into a corset that's stronger than owt I put across Peggy's back ... then walk all the way to Egremont to sit in the picture house in the dark where no one can see her, just because she reckons she looks smarter and years younger,' continued Jackson, ignoring Tom's remark. 'It takes sheer strength of will to suffer like that Tom.'

'Well, I reckon I'll have to get myself into Egremont to see the doctor if I'm no better by tomorrow morning. It costs me money to be ill, maybe a few tablets'll put things right.'

'Suit yourself Tom, but I remember years ago when we were farming at Gosforth, I woke up with an awful bad back, just like yours.'

'Did you cure it?' asked Tom hopefully as he eased his back from the door jamb to a more comfortable spot against the byre wall.

Jackson opened his mouth to reply but was interrupted by the sound of the byre door opening.

'I thought I saw you limping this way Tom, what on earth is wrong with you . . . ?'

'I thought that for once someone had managed to get past the kitchen window without having to undergo a medical check-up!'

'Not so much of your cheek Jackson!' retorted Edith sharply, 'And why have you not offered him a seat? The poor chap has stood leaning against that wall for at least fifteen minutes.'

'Don't be so daft woman, you'd think I didn't know a thing about a bad back! I know damned fine that if he sat himself down on one of them milking copies I'd break me own back trying to lift him off again. A chap's better stopping on his feet as long as he can . . . just like a working horse . . . once it's down on its knees it's finished . . .'

'Come on into the house Tom, we've a good upright chair near the fire that'll suit you fine.'

'Jackson was just about to tell me how he healed his back years ago.'

'Well, come on in Tom, Jackson tells his tales better in the kitchen where the rest of us can suffer in warmth and comfort.'

Jackson snorted his disapproval.

'You'd think I told folks lies Edith.'

He shut the door firmly then continued his explanation.

'No, not lies Tom, just the truth . . . but a tale isn't worth the telling if it can be written on the back of a postcard.'

'And since when did you ever write or send any postcards?' asked Edith as she led the way across the yard to the back door.

'Our relatives in the south of the country and in the Lakes wouldn't know if we were still alive or dead if it wasn't for me and the other women in the family sitting down and writing a letter or two. God only knows what most men did when they were in school because it couldn't have been Writing lessons.'

She made her way into the kitchen and lifted the steaming kettle off the cheerful fire.

'I was like a lot more lads, I'd never seen my father write anything other than bills and sign cheques . . . and we always managed to be clothed and fed . . . besides most women like to sit down and write a letter or two. I think Tom, they enjoy writing about who has died and who has been born. I don't think our Edith would know that we've had a litter of new ferrets or that the corn was a bit thin this year in that field near the station.'

'Who on earth would be interested in that Jackson? I look forward to getting a reply . . . we'd soon be cut off from our relatives if I wrote something that read as though it had been written for the "Farmer's Weekly".'

Tom laughed, then gasped in pain.

'Oh! My back Edith! I'm not so good at laughing, but I'd welcome a mug of tea thanks!'

'Tea isn't the answer Tom, now just you listen to me.'

The friends were now settled by the fire as Jackson began his story.

'My God I was bad that day Tom! Edith had to help

with the morning's milking and you know how useless she is when she gets within tail-swishing distance of a cow. Well, as the day wore on I thought that I'd just potter slowly across the field towards Gosforth village . . . just to loosen things up at bit.'

'It's a strange thing Tom, but he only made it as far as the first pub.'

'You forget Mother, that's the first spot you come to where you can get a sit down . . . I was buggered Tom . . . as you'll understand.'

Tom nodded in painful agreement.

'Believe it or not, just as I was on the point of going into the pub for a quiet sit down . . .'

He glared in Edith's direction, he'd heard her chuckling as she started to clear the table.

'. . . a quiet sit down' he repeated tetchily '. . . when suddenly a gipsy-looking woman came out of a cottage doorway nearby. She was begging as usual, so I gave her a copper or two.'

'Lucky she caught you as you were going *into* the pub,' laughed Edith, '. . . or, like me, she might have had the devil of a job to see the colour of your money if she'd waited until you came out!'

Jackson ignored his wife's observation and continued addressing a perplexed Tom, unsure of the direction of his friend's tale.

'Like I said, she was a gipsy, and as I was leaning heavily on my stick all the time I was talking to her she must have noticed my bad rheumatics, "thanks for the money Mister" she said "but I see you have the rheumatics very bad" I told her she was right about that. "I can give you a cure" she said.'

'Was it any good?' asked a hopeful Tom.

'Aye that it was.'

'What did she tell you to do Jackson?'

'She told me that the cure the gypsies swore by was . . .' and here Jackson spit expertly into the back of the hot fireplace, then listened approvingly as the fire hissed its annoyance. Tom wriggled in painful anticipation.

'. . . celery, that's what she said Tom . . . celery . . . eat plenty of celery!'

'Did it work?'

'Oh, aye! Look at me now . . . I've never suffered from rheumatics from that day to this!'

'That's why I always grow a row or two of celery every year. It just keeps things going in the right direction.'

'I always wondered why you are about the only farmer in this district that grows celery. Good God Jackson, I'll start on celery as soon as I get back home.'

'You'll notice Tom, that you never hear a word in the "Farmers' Weekly" about the curative qualities of celery. You can't expect them to know something that's been handed down from generation to generation. You know Tom, them gipsies never waste time in school learning to read and write, they manage very well without it . . . have you ever seen a gipsy hobbling about, propping himself up against a byre wall?'

'I guess I haven't.'

'No, they're too busy scrounging about seeing what they can steal when your back's turned,' observed Edith tartly, '. . . and, what's more, schools don't really like having their dirty children mixing among the nice clean pupils . . . the mothers are bothered about them catching lice.' She shivered as she spoke.

'There's a good example of Christian charity for you Tom! You'd think lice were immortal or something! The ones I caught . . . in school, mind you . . . died quickly enough when my mother got on their tracks! Besides, this gipsy wasn't as concerned with money as you might think.'

'What makes you say that Jackson, she was quick enough to take your money, wasn't she?'

'But Edith I didn't finish my tale. You shouldn't jump to conclusions!'

'Go on then, let's hear how she returned your money . . . with interest!' laughed Edith as she began to prepare the vegetables for the dinner.

'It was a year later, almost to the day, when I saw her again. I was as fit as I've always been. Of course I wanted to give her something for such a good cure, so I handed her a £1 note, reckoning that it was little enough to repay her for all the pain she saved me from. But to my amazement she refused to take the note! "I never take money for cures," she said, "but if you'd buy a pair of these shoe laces, I'd be really grateful Sir." '

Jackson leaned forward to poke the fire, nodding his head sagely.

'A good cheap cure, wouldn't you say Tom? I bet the doctor couldn't provide a cure for the price of a pair of shoelaces.'

'Don't be foolish enough to copy our Jackson, . . . celery mightn't do the trick for you Tom . . . I'd get somebody to run you to Egremont for the evening surgery . . . you can't be too sure about a bad back.'

Tom nodded slowly, pondering the quandary.

'I'd rather give the celery a try Edith, I never grow it but I'm sure you have some you could give me to try out. It's a bit quicker than waiting in the doctor's for an hour or so, it can't do a bad back much good to sit on them hard benches . . . and then to stand in a queue in the chemist's for long enough. No, I'll give the celery a try, then if I'm no better next week I'll go in to the surgery.'

'That's a sensible decision Tom, it's no good struggling there and run the risk of making youself worse, just to please the women.'

'I've never heard such rubbish,' snapped Edith in exasperation.

'The assistants in the chemist's are very kind, they

always offer me a chair to sit on while I wait for my prescription to be made up.'

'Aye, they like to please the women, they know that they rely on them to keep the business flourishing! Most of us would stay at home and fight it, but since this new Health Service started they're all waiting with their hands out for the easy money that they get from our taxes . . . believe me Tom, they have a eye for a quick penny.'

'I don't know how you can say that Jackson, you, who's never needed a doctor in your life . . . you should be the last to pass judgement.'

'Maybe I've never needed a doctor in my life, but I listen to them that go there regular like. I was listening to Alan Steel talking about a friend of theirs . . . one of them women who's never away from the doctor's door . . .'

'What tale was that?'

'I'm just about to tell you Edith, if you'll give time! She was sitting, like you say, on one of them chairs in the chemist's shop waiting for one of them new-fangled prescriptions to be made up for her rheumatics . . . when a helpful assistant with nothing better to do . . . asked her if she'd ever tried a copper bangle as a cure. "No, never," the woman replied . . . then the assistant whipped a couple of dozen of them from under the counter to try.'

'Did she buy one?' asked an unsurprised Tom.

'Of course she did . . . after all Tom, a wise person takes all the advice that's offered.'

'But, she'd just been to the doctor for advice! They have a cheek selling other cures in the chemist's.'

'They've done that for years Edith as you well know, they're not going to change now. I've noticed that it's the same with the veterinary medicines they sell. The same cure does for . . . coughs, the skitters or hardpad

. . . it's all the same . . . they make their money whatever happens to the patient.'

'I wonder if the copper bangle worked?' mused Tom.

'I should try the celery first if I were you Tom,' advised Jackson.

'If it fails no-one will be any the wiser . . . but if you go around wearing a gold bracelet round your wrist, they'll reckon you've gone a bit soft in the head . . . or somewhere else!'

Tom laughed in agreement and slowly began to rise to his feet, then paused as he remembered why he had come.

'Oh, I almost forgot the liniment that Mary said you had rubbed onto your back. It would be a good idea to try more than one thing at a time . . . and it can't do any harm I don't suppose.'

'I'll get you a bottle,' said Edith as she reached up to the medicine cupboard. To Tom's surprise Jackson began to chuckle.

'Now that's just where you're wrong Tom. You'll find that a chap with a bad back can't rub the bloody stuff on by himself.'

'Mary'll be good enough to put it on for me Jackson, we'll manage all right . . . I can't see what's so funny about . . .'

'. . . it's only funny now when it's all over Tom! It was like this . . . I gave the bottle to Edith to rub into the bottom of my spine . . . and she was as good as her word . . . she rubbed it in, but she put too much into her hand . . . and the bloody burning stuff trickled down into my . . .'

'. . . the Fiery Jack was too thin . . . how was I to know it stung like that Tom?' interrupted Edith quickly.

'Stung? Stung! It was worse than the pain in my back! I reckon the manufacturers put the same stuff in the bottles with ''Horse Liniment'' on the label. I tell you it's a mistake to buy anything in that chemist's.'

'To tell you the truth Tom, he had a job to sit down for a day or so! Just you warn Mary about being careful when she pours it into her hand.'

Tom pushed the offending liniment into his pocket as he tried unsuccessfully to straighten his body, then grinned at his two advisers.

'Well. I'm off! I'm not a bit sure about these cures, but I'll try the celery, it seems less painful . . . if it doesn't work right away, I'll be back for a good tasty celery recipe or two . . . I don't fancy a diet of raw celery every day!'

'What on earth does he want?' snapped Jackson as soon as the door had closed behind his friend, '. . . not only does he get a cure for nowt . . . he expects us to make it tasty for him as well! He doesn't ail enough if you ask me!'

2

MARIE COMES

Jackson crossed the farmyard making his way towards the solid sandstone barn. He pushed the heavy door open and waited while his eyes became accustomed to the darkness. After a pause he walked to his boxes of seed potatoes stacked up in the far corner away from any possible draughts. He lifted the light layer of straw which lay on top of them and examined them closely as he had done regularly throughout the winter. The potato boxes allowed the air to circulate above and below as well as around their contents thus keeping them as healthy as possible during the dark, damp winter weather.

This clear April morning was just right for a day's potato setting. The field had been prepared, the stitches well mucked to provide a good deep bed with plenty for the seed potatoes to feed on, just like a nice tight sandwich . . . thought Jackson . . . all he asked of them was that they should grow.

Potatoes had always been his best cash crop, but at what cost! Each potato had already been picked, sorted and then carefully examined throughout the winter for any damage. Each one must have been handled at least six times, and now they faced the last stage . . . a careful planting by hand. The sprouts were vigorous, a fitting testimony to his observation and care throughout the winter. It should be a good crop this year . . . provided the weather was kind. He turned towards the farmhouse hoping everybody was ready to lend a hand, potato setting was one of those jobs that could be finished quickly if there was plenty of willing hands.

* * *

'I'm pleased to see you so busy this morning Esther, you must have remembered that we'll have to be off early today if we're to get them taties set in good time,' said Jackson encouragingly to his daughter as he sat down to breakfast.

'I'm clearing the table early because Marie is coming from Cleator Moor this morning, she's managed to get a lift and should be here soon.'

'It's nice that Esther has such a nice friend who bothers to come all this way to spend a day or two with us.'

'But it's a busy time of the year Mother, we can't spare Esther to go gallivanting about the countryside admiring the view when there's taties to be set, muck to be led and stock to be seen to. The cows don't stop giving milk just because we're busy in the fields. Why can't visitors come in the bad weather when we've plenty of time to talk to them?'

'But Marie is coming to help us to work in the fields Dad. Didn't you say you wanted us to take some seed potatoes to the field and then to set them? Marie says she fancies helping us for a day or so. There's nothing to do as interesting as that on Cleator Moor . . . or so she says.'

'I've always liked Marie. She's a lass with the right ideas. Most folk on Cleator Moor like eating taties but have little notion about how they get into the bags. Yes, Esther, she'll learn a lot today.'

'I thought you'd be pleased. She'll be here any minute.'

'Well, you can get yourself outside and put Jewel in the cart . . . remember to put the shelvings on, we need to pile the tatie boxes on top of them to make a decent load.'

'I know what to do, you'd think I'd been brought up in

a town Dad! I thought we might have taken Peggy, she's very reliable and can be trusted to stand still while we load her . . . Jewel can still be a bit skittish when she chooses.'

Jackson looked up in annoyance.

'I know half the countryside still call her the *flying horse* after that daft carry-on when we first bought her . . . but I've taught her a few manners since then. After all I couldn't let the neighbours think that I can't control one of my horses . . . she'll stand on that road as docile as Peggy while you two strong lasses load her cart.'

Esther nodded in agreement as she heard her friend cross the farmyard to the noisy greetings of the two dogs.

'And . . . don't forget to load those two bags of artificial manure in first or you'll never manage to lift them over the wide shelvings. You've got to show these townsfolk the proper way to load a cart. And just you think on to be careful about knocking them sprouts. I haven't spent the entire winter nursing them seed taties for you to upset them on their last day above ground!'

Marie settled herself at the table eager to sample the hot tea and breakfast which had been prepared for her.

'You tackle that ham as though you haven't eaten for a week Marie.'

'Well, Uncle Jackson, I had to leave the house early this morning so I hadn't time to eat much . . . but I always know that there'll be a good meal waiting for me as soon as I get here.'

'And I hear that you're going to help us today Lass.'

'Of course, I've always wanted to learn more about how a farm works. I've only helped at hay and harvest time, so I want to know what happens early in the year, at sowing time.'

'A good idea.' Jackson nodded approvingly. 'You've come to the right spot today. We have a lot of hard work in front of us . . . you'll be jiggered by teatime and you can go back to Cleator Moor and tell them what hard work it is feeding the townsfolk in the district.'

'I will . . . but I'm a little nervous of your big horses . . . they are so high up, and have such big feet . . . and mouths that are always chewing something.'

Jackson laughed. 'It's only a bridle bit in their mouth . . . unless they had a good strong bit in their mouth we would have no control over them at all. But, you know Marie, my horses are so well trained that the bridle and bit don't matter very much . . . they are all obedient . . . you just have to shout at them and they obey straight away . . . it's only a matter of kindness and training . . . now don't you worry about a thing . . . our horses will look after you.'

Soon the two friends were heaving the bags of artificial manure into the cart while Jewel waited patiently for them to finish the loading.

'That's the hardest part over Marie. Those bags were heavy. As soon as we get the shelvings on we can start loading those boxes of seed potatoes onto the cart. They're nice and light to lift, we have to be careful we don't knock the sprouts off.'

'Mmm . . . those sprouts look very strong, you should get a good crop from them Esther.'

'Spoken like a true farmer Marie!'

The two girls were soon ensconced in the cart surrounded by the wide shelvings on which they began to place the boxes which were passed up to them by Jackson.

'Keep that little gap clear at the front Marie, so the reins can be reached . . . we've got to stay on board until we get to the field and I'll drive the horse from the space left in the middle of the cart inside the ring of boxes.'

'I never thought about that, but we'll have to steer the horse somehow I suppose. Couldn't your dad lead the horse and we can ride inside?'

'I suppose he could, but I think he's bringing Peggy

with a load of muck along as well so it saves him having to walk back for it. It's all to save extra work Marie.'

'Yes, we can manage, over breakfast your dad was telling me that Jewel is a very obedient horse. I don't feel as nervous as I thought I might.'

The boxes began to rise around the girls, and Marie began to feel as though she was being trapped in the middle of the load. She turned to Esther for reassurance.

'I'm beginning to feel as though I'm being trapped in this cart Esther, I hope Jewel walks slowly when we set off, I think I might topple onto those delicate potatoes.'

'Don't worry Marie, Jewel is bound to walk slowly, I don't think she'll fancy racing along with a huge load like this one behind her.'

Esther smiled to herself as she remembered how flighty Jewel had been when she had first come to the farm and how difficult it had been to keep her in the fields. Her thoughts were suddenly interrupted by Marie's nervous voice.

'What's Jewel doing Esther? She's rubbing her head on her leg . . . can you reach the reins if she decides to walk away?'

Esther smiled confidently and reached for the reins which were hanging over the front of the cart and lying on the floor.

'Yes, I can reach them alright Marie . . . just pass that box coming up on your side.'

Suddenly the box was wrenched out of Marie's reaching arms as the cart jolted violently forward.

'Grab the reins Esther!' called Jackson as he realised that his horse was taking off at a smart gallop.

Esther pulled furiously at the reins, but found no resistance. She gazed in dismay at the flying mane and the horse's head, bare as the day she was born! Jewel had rubbed her bridle off! The minute she had seen the wide load behind her she had panicked and bolted, hoping to gallop to freedom.

Esther knew of the horse's jumping prowess and had visions of the mare having a go at leaping the hedges to escape from the menace at her tail. What should she do? Her father was now far behind.

Marie clung as best she could to whatever was to hand, but the potato boxes she tried to cling to were rattling off the shelvings and scattering their precious contents along the roadway.

'Jump when you can free yourself,' Esther called to the terrified Marie, thinking that if the cart was over-turned they might be trapped under it and seriously injured.

Both girls seemed to find a strength they were unaware of as first a terrified Marie and then an equally terrified Esther executed a standing jump over the wide shelvings praying that their landing would inflict as little damage to them as possible.

The two friends painfully gathered themselves up from the unwelcoming road just in time to see Jewel and her trailing shelvings disappear round the next bend with Jackson in hot, cursing pursuit.

*   *   *

'I have no idea what I'm going to say to your mother Marie when she sees you coming home with your arm in a sling!'

'But, what about my sling?'

'Your injury doesn't matter Esther, you've always known what dangers there are on a farm, but Marie's mother thought she would be safe for a few days with us.'

'Well, there's no bones broken, so she won't say anything,' replied Marie firmly. 'It's all part of farm life I suppose, I'll be able to tell the story to all my friends . . .'

'I hope you won't! Jackson'll have to do these dangerous jobs himself in future . . . I can't understand

him letting you work with a temperamental beast like Jewel.'

'Yes, Dad says if she was a singer she would be a primadonna, because she's so unpredictable.'

'For goodness sake stop saying such things . . . you go from bad to worse. And tonight is the night Jackson goes to the Grey Mare, I just hope nobody has heard of the accident!'

Esther laughed.

'The whole neighbourhood will have heard by now, they'll be waiting for him in the Grey Mare like a pack of hungry wolves. He won't be able to talk himself out of this so easily . . . but he had to go . . . said he would put things straight before anybody circulated any lies and malicious gossip around the district!'

* * *

The door closed behind Alan Steel as he entered the Grey Mare and shook the rain from his cap in disgust.

'Started to rain at last . . . it's threatened rain all day, thank God I've managed to get that twenty acre field set with taties today.'

Jackson grunted scarcely glancing up from his dominoes.

'You've been lucky then,' agreed Tom Graham genially as he perused his hand.

'Surely everybody in the district could see the rain coming and would get on with their spring sowing,' continued Alan conversationally, '. . . old-timers like you Jackson wouldn't waste a minute of a fine day like today.'

'No, he didn't waste a minute of it like you say,' agreed Tom, '. . . but didn't you hear that there was a bit of an accident on Jackson's farm today?'

Alan looked genuinely perplexed.

'No, I didn't hear anything . . . I hope nobody's hurt, Jackson looks OK to me.'

'I took Esther and her friend Marie to hospital in my car, but they're both fine, no bones broken . . . just a nasty sprain and bruises.'

'What on earth happened?'

'I knew if I didn't come in here myself there would be some garbled account of a simple accident . . .'

'Well, let's all hear about the simple accident then,' urged Bill Brown lowering his dominoes, sensing a tale that wouldn't be to the old farmer's advantage.

'It was nothing . . . just showing a visitor a bit about farm life . . . it's always a danger having strangers on a farm upsetting the stock with their town ways.'

Alan laughed at the old man's nerve.

'From what Tom has just said, you very nearly killed the lasses. You don't go to hospital for no good reason.'

'Hospital! It wasn't my idea that they should go traipsing off to the hospital . . . you know how women fuss over a little bump.'

'Edith was right Jackson, it's always best to make sure that there isn't a fracture . . . the likes of us are not to know . . . it was no trouble for me to run them down to Whitehaven.'

'Nobody has asked me how the horse is I notice.'

As soon as he said the words Jackson realised his mistake.

'Don't say one of your horses caused an accident.'

'They were loading boxes of seed potatoes onto the cart when the horse decided to bolt . . .'

'Yes Tom, that sounds like it . . . and I bet it wasn't Peggy . . . she's too well-bred to misbehave like that . . . she had her goodness bred in the bone! It would be that mare that he's been training like a circus dancing horse ever since the day he was daft enough to buy it cheap at Wigton.'

'She managed to rub her bridle off then panicked and

bolted,' added Tom hoping he could redirect any uncomplimentary remarks that might be coming his friend's way.

'So the horse bolted and the girls got thrown out then?'

'Aye, they did.'

'So what happened to the horse? I expect it's either still running or Jackson has had the good sense to shoot it!'

'Neither,' snorted Jackson riled by the comments. 'You weren't to know that there were two bags of heavy manure in the bottom of the cart which slid to the back as she galloped.'

'What difference did that make then Jackson?' laughed Alan delighted by the news, and eager to hear more of the unhappy escapade.

Jackson by now was recovering quickly from his disadvantageous stance.

'If you'll only listen for a minute you'll hear the truth of today's little skirmish.'

'Fine, I'll just order my pint . . . and if you can convince me that it was all just an unfortunate mishap, I'll buy you the next drink.'

Jackson settled himself in his usual chair and glanced around the waiting faces.

'Horses are not machines like a motor car that you can leave out of gear while you load them up.'

'We all know that.'

'You said you'd listen,' snapped Jackson, '. . . so you'd better keep quiet if you want to hear the truth . . . like you have already rightly said, Peggy is one on her own, I can't expect a mare that I haven't bred myself to behave as well she does. It takes time to undo other folks' mistakes and you've got to trust the horse a bit as you go along. Of one thing I'm sure . . . that mare won't do that again.'

'How can you be so sure of that? After all, she got away with it today.'

'Most horses take fright if they suddenly see a wide load behind them. If she hadn't rubbed her bridle off we wouldn't be talking nonsense here.'

'That won't stop her doing it again Jackson, surely?' volunteered Bill Brown.

'. . . but that's where you're wrong Bill . . . you never let me tell you what happened to the mare.'

'That's right,' agreed Tom, '. . . go on Jackson, tell them about when you caught up to her.'

'Aye, above five miles away if you asked me!'

'No, it wasn't very far at all. I caught up to her hanging in the air! The heavy bags of artificial manure had shuffled to the back of the cart and had tipped the shafts up . . . lifting the daft mare with them! If I hadn't reached her quickly she would have hanged herself with her collar . . . which she was swinging on . . . like a highwayman on a gibbet in the olden times.'

'My God! I would have given a gold sovereign to see a sight like that Jackson,' laughed Alan.

'I thought about leaving the stupid bugger hanging where she was . . . she's been nowt but trouble ever since I bought her.'

'That's a change of tune Jackson . . .'

'I only cut her down because that agent from the railway in Whitehaven called in last week to see if I had anything big and strong to sell him to work in the goods yard. He usually looks for a big gelding. He saw that black bugger and fancied her, but likely he thought I might want to breed from her.'

'That's about the best thing to do with her Jackson,' nodded Tom in approval.

'No, I reckon not. With the temperament she's got I can't imagine her letting me lock her foal in the stable while she works in the fields. The stupid bugger would make off for the gate every time a chap stopped for a chew of tobacco or went for a bit of relief in the dyke back.'

A titter greeted the last observation.

'You'd have to spend less time drinking in here if you have a long day's work looking at you the next day . . . and you daren't stop for a bit of relief,' laughed Bill Brown gleefully.

'I've given the matter some thought . . .' continued Jackson, ignoring the remark. '. . . I think she'd probably do well in Whitehaven.'

'What about the traffic? She might bolt in the middle of the street and do a lot of damage . . . maybe kill somebody . . . a bit of a dangerous move if you ask me,' observed Alan thoughtfully.

'Trust you to think of something daft like that Alan. Them chaps who work on the railway can handle horses as well as anyone sitting in here. I won't sell her without letting them know what she's like . . . I'll give them more help than I ever got when I put good money down for her. Oh! no! she'll be all right with them. Once they know she can't be trusted they'll yoke her with a good well-behaved horse like our Peggy and she'll work well in a draught. She'll not run very far with one of them big-boned geldings tied to her bridle . . . and a heavy load fastened behind her. Yes, I think that would be a very satisfactory deal.'

'Do you know Jackson, if you fell into the beck you'd come out with your pockets full of fish!' laughed Bill.

'Luck has nothing to do with it Bill . . . speculation is what it's all about. I think the visit from Marie today has just pointed my mind in the right direction! Maybe I'll spend a day at Wigton soon and see if anybody has a good strong horse going cheap, that I can tutor a bit.'

'If you don't kill either yourself or someone more important in the meantime,' muttered Alan to himself. Aloud he said, 'Well, I suppose I owe you a pint for a reasonable defence ... but you still have to explain things to Marie's mother.'

'Marie's mother is like a lot of women who live in town and spend their week-ends watching them cowboy pictures ... she'll think a farm is a bit like a rodeo ... and that her lass has got off pretty lightly with only a sprained wrist to show after all the excitement!'

The bar of the Grey Mare resounded to the quiet laughter of the regulars who once more felt that the wily old farmer had tried to pull the wool over their eyes!

3

BULLS

'**G**ood God!' exclaimed Edith, her shocked voice wakening Jackson from his evening doze.

'What on earth's the matter with you woman? Has somebody we know died?'

'No, not exactly, but I'm just reading this account in the "Whitehaven News" . . .'

'Serves you right for bothering to read news that's a week old . . . whatever's wrong'll be put right by now.'

'No, it says that John Batty from Gosforth was nearly gored to death last week by a bull . . .'

'What breed was it Edith?'

'Let me see . . . yes, it was an Ayrshire . . .'

'There you are then, that was his first mistake. The second was that he must have let his attention wander. Bulls are always unpredictable, but I wouldn't give a stall in my byre to an Ayrshire bull. That's just asking for trouble!'

'I don't see how you can say such things Jackson, you've kept bulls that weren't Ayrshires and were bad enough to deal with.'

'I can't agree with that Edith, you take a risk with any bull you keep, but to buy a bull from a breed that's a known killer . . . well you have only yourself to blame. Pass me the paper so that I can read for myself what the daft bugger did.'

Edith passed the newspaper to her disgruntled husband. The farmer chuckled softly to himself as he read the article. Edith tossed her head in exasperation as she heard the chuckles.

'I don't see what's funny about such a horrible incident Jackson, he was nearly killed and think of the problems he will have now when he's not fit to work for a while. Maybe some kind neighbour will give him a few days work and see them through this hard patch. I hear his wife has just had a baby too . . . it must be a worrying time for them.'

She nodded her head in sympathy as she began to set the table for supper.

Suddenly Jackson laughed out loud.

'Here just listen to this . . . "the farmer was saved from a severe goring because the bull's horns were so long and curved that he was trapped against the barn wall without them piercing him too badly." '

'Thank God! You see Jackson, a bull with shorter horns like ours would probably have killed him.'

'You might be right at that Edith, but them Ayrshires are born with a malicious streak. You've seen them in the arenas, bullfighting in Spain haven't you? Bullfighters know which breeds are vicious by nature.'

'They aren't the same breeds there, they're black with long curved horns.'

'They must be related in some way Edith, after all there were only two cows that went into the Ark with Noah, so they must have developed on the same lines since then.'

'You twist everything to suit your own point of view Jackson, I have no patience with you. I feel so sorry for John and his wife.'

'There you go again, the Bible knows all the answers, until it comes to something a bit technical, like breeds of animals, then you holy folks get all confused and talk about the will of God and such-like rubbish. The chap made too many mistakes when he should have known better. I bet his father never got himself pinned up against a wall and shouting for mercy! No, he would have his mind on what he was doing, not day-dreaming about a new baby or some such daftness.'

Edith rapped the table as she placed the mugs down,

her exasperation irritating her husband, who continued to read with great relish.

'Just you thank God you've never been in such a situation.'

'I call tell you another true story about keeping unsuitable bulls and taking daft chances,' said Jackson lowering his newspaper.

A rattle of the back door coupled with the excited barking of the dogs heralded the arrival of a visitor.

'It'll be Tom,' said Edith. 'Don't go on about how stupid John has been with his bull, your remarks might just get back to him.'

'Next time I see him in the auction at Whitehaven I'll tell him to his face what a bloody fool he's been.'

'Who's been a bloody fool Jackson?'

'Come in Tom, I've been reading about that goring incident at Gosforth.'

'Yes, I've read about it this afternoon, a sad affair that might have been a tragedy. We could all be in that situation any day Jackson, it's only a matter of luck.'

'That's just what Jackson was saying,' added Edith quickly, sensing a clash of opinion, 'I'm sure you would like a cup of tea and a piece of this seed cake that I made earlier this afternoon.'

'I was just about to tell our Edith another true story about a bull Tom.'

'A true one Jackson?'

'Of course it's a true story, I'm not as good at telling lies as you might think. Another thing Tom . . . true stories are the best, they have that special ring to them.'

'True enough . . . what is the story? I can't think of any other incident of a bull goring its owner or handler that we haven't talked about before.'

'This was a true tale I was told one day at a horse sale in Wigton. A chap there was buying a horse and was telling me that he'd had a bit of bad luck with a Jersey bull.'

He paused to reach for his piece of cake to keep his listener waiting.

'Now that's a breed I know nowt about Jackson.'

'Aye, well this chap didn't seem to know so much about it either. Jersey bulls are perhaps the most vicious you can keep.'

'It's a breed that's well known for producing a high fat content in the milk,' said Edith knowledgeably.

'That's a good example of somebody who lives and works with farm stock and only knows one or two money-making facts about them.'

Tom laughed. 'I know that much as well Jackson . . . tell us what you know then.'

'Like I was saying, this chap had a bit of money to throw about, he had that sort of accent. A chap who talks fancy usually has more money than sense.'

Edith clicked her tongue in annoyance.

'Folks are getting better educated these days and know how to speak well. You shouldn't judge people in that way Jackson.'

'Education? education? it's like some of them local farmers' sons who have gone to study at that college near Penrith . . . what is it called?'

'Newton Rigg.'

'Aye, that's the spot. They come back with fancy time-wasting ideas about how to wash cows before you milk them . . . and how everything has to be weighed and measured to prove that you're making progress. Daftness, I call it. I've always known if things were getting better or worse without buying expensive equipment to measure either my progress or my losses. A rule of thumb measurement saves a lot of heartache. If things are going a bit wrong then it's getting better before I notice how bad it was.'

'Such an outlook stops any sort of progress, don't take any notice of him Tom, he talks the way his mouth stands.'

'I'm waiting to hear about this fancy-talking stranger you met at Wigton.'

'If some folk would keep quiet I'd be finished by now,' he laughed. 'Like I was saying he was there to buy a horse. He had a small farm near Penrith and had kept some Jersey cows and a good Jersey bull. Milk for the upper classes you know Tom! Well, one day a neighbour who fancied he could improve his milk cheque by serving a few of his decent Friesian heifers with this chap's Jersey bull asked if he could borrow it for a few weeks.'

'What's wrong with that Jackson, it seems like a good move to me.'

'Aye, it would have been if the chap with the Freisians hadn't been a breeder of Tamworth pigs.'

'What difference could that make?'

'Just you listen Edith and you'll find out. This chap had his fancy pigs running free in a field, he must have read about pigs running wild and making better eating,' snorted Jackson in disdain. 'A load of rubbish if you have to chase the bloody things around the countryside to do owt with them, let alone the weight they can lose dancing about. They talk about tough bacon, well that's the way to grow it!'

'Come on Jackson, finish your tale.'

'As I said, he had all this livestock running about in a big field near the farmhouse. So he put the Jersey bull he'd borrowed in the same field as the pigs and the young heifers so that he could keep an eye on them, silly bugger!'

'I can't see what's wrong with keeping an eye on your stock Jackson.'

'Aye, well, you don't know a lot about breeding stock Edith. The daft chap decided to put some feed in a trough for the pigs. Likely he thought that the bull would be content to graze even when it could smell something better in the trough.'

'Maybe the grazing was poor and the bull was hungry?' ventured Edith sympathetically.

'Maybe, but if you're daft enough to put tasty food in a trough thinking that the stock can read your mind and work out that it was only intended for some of them and not others, then you're asking for trouble. Maybe he thought he should have put a notice on . . . THIS MEAL IS FOR PIGS ONLY . . . but knowing they can't read he left it up to the animals to work things out.'

'What happened then Jackson?'

'Well Tom, the pigs made a dash for the trough and got stuck in. Then the bull noticed that something interesting was on the menu, so he made his way over to make sure he got his share. Of course he was used to getting his own way and pushing any other stock out of the way. The boar gave him a warning grunt or two, but the bull wasn't going to be put off by a smaller animal who had the cheek to threaten him, so he tucked in along with the rest of the pigs.'

'What happened then?' asked Edith beginning to feel that something very unpleasant was about to happen to one of the protagonists.

'The chap told me that the boar was enraged at the bull's invasion of his territory and turned and in a flash attacked the bull with its tusks. In a second he had dashed under the bull's belly and ripped it from one end to the other. The bull was dead in seconds. He said that the boar's tusk had sawed through the ribs as neatly as any butcher could have done.'

'What a terrible thing to happen!' said a shocked Edith '. . . the poor man must have been beside himself.'

'Not half as much as the owner of the bull, who was only doing the neighbour a good turn.'

'Aye, you've got to know what you're doing if you take to breeding rare breeds Jackson.'

'That's why they're so bloody rare Tom, they're just a nuisance to have around if they can't be managed alongside ordinary stock. Domestic breeds can be hard enough as the incident at Gosforth shows. A chap has to be master on his own farm or else things get out of hand.'

'But there's no need for cruelty, animals like to live outside and enjoy a bit of freedom and fresh air.'

'There you go Tom, listen to that sort of daft talk, it's typical of someone brought up in a town, they think of animals as though they could make decisions and form an opinion about life like us human beings can. The next thing Edith'll be telling us is that animals enjoy the view and like to choose which fields they want to graze in! Rubbish I call it, a good farmer knows the value of a strong door and solid gates so that the stock knows where they live and who's in charge.'

'Well, I just hope you never make a mistake Jackson, there's such a thing as over-confidence.'

'Not on my farm Edith, in my yard the farmer has to be the boss, otherwise I'd be scared to handle any animal which shakes its head at me.'

He turned to Tom, 'I expect you've come to castrate my bull calves, Tom?'

'That's right Jackson.'

'Aye, well, that's a good start for the day and will stop them getting any bullfighting notions!'

Edith shook her head and smiled to herself as the two men left the fireside. Humility wasn't one of her husband's strong points of that she was certain!

4

AUNT MAY TAKES A HOLIDAY

The sweat trickled down Jackson's face as he drove the unwilling horses back for the last time before dinner towards the roadside dyke. Once Peggy and Captain realised that a dinner break was imminent they heaved the mowing machine briskly in the direction of the field gate.

Jackson mopped his brow with his soggy cap and pulled the eager pair backwards in order to unfasten their chains. 'I can't blame them' he thought to himself, 'this bloody heatwave is killing the lot of us.'

When Jackson and his two happy homeward bound horses moved onto the baking tarmac of the narrow road, the air became even more oppressive. The sultry atmosphere reeked of a mix of horse sweat, newly mown grass and the heady scent of the wild summer roses and honeysuckle which flourished in the deep hedgerows. The buzz of busy insects gathering pollen added a sense of light dizziness to the lazy air. Tired and footsore, Jackson was pleased when he reached his yard gate.

To the horses' annoyance they were led, on arrival, straight into their stable instead of drinking the yard trough dry.

'You two, you never seem to remember that we never let you drink when you're sweating. I don't want you struggling with colic.' You'd think nature would tell them what was dangerous! But ... he thought to himself as he filled their troughs with crushed oats mixed with chopped turnips ... I reckon *we're* no better, we tend to do whatever we fancy without working out the consequences . . . and humans are supposed to be superior beings. God! But it was a hot day . . . maybe an hour or so in the house would let both him and the horses have a good rest before returning to the uncut ground.

'Come and have a sit down Jackson,' said Edith as he made he way to his seat at the kitchen table.

'. . . I've some lovely boiled ham and taties ready.'

'Don't mention the word *boiled* to me today Edith, I feel like a roasted pig and those two horses have been lathered up since we started out this morning.'

'Poor creatures, they shouldn't be required to work in this hot sun, it's nothing short of cruel; the hay would grow a bit longer if you waited until we had a cooler day.'

'My God Edith! What do you think we are running here? A holiday home for knackered workhorses?'

'No, but they are only flesh and blood like us. If you are suffering they must be suffering too.'

'But that's what I bought them for! To do the work that I can't do! Likely you wouldn't bat an eye if I pulled the bloody mowing machine up and down the field . . . I suppose that wouldn't be cruel?' He asked tetchily. 'You're like a lot more of these animal lovers . . . you think the animals would treat you in exactly the same way . . . but just you stop and think about it for a minute Edith . . .'

Edith pushed a plate of pudding roughly in her husband's direction, her hand shaking with exasperation.

'You twist everything I say Jackson, you know perfectly well that the animals have no choice in the matter, but *you* can stop if you feel ill.'

Jackson paused as he tackled his sponge pudding. 'Now just think for a minute about that bloody lazy cat sitting on the window ledge ready to move the minute the sun leaves it in the shade . . .'

'Don't be so silly, a cat isn't a beast of burden like the horses. It's not the same thing at all.'

Now it was Jackson's turn to show exasperation.

'Just le me finish what I was saying . . . see that cute little cat snoozing as happy as a sand boy while the rats and mice sun bathe on the barn roof, knowing damned well that they can sleep safely all afternoon . . . they only have to look down here to know that they're as safe as houses.'

'Tell me what all this *cat* conversation is about, I'm lost already.'

'It's straightforward . . . if you'll just be quiet and listen I'll explain a bit of animal psychology to you.'

Edith smiled to herself, but kept quiet in order to hear how he could talk himself out of her cruelty charge.

Jackson leant back in his comfortable chair and waved his arm expansively in the direction of the sleeping cat.

'Just you imagine if things were reversed Edith. What if we all changed shape, like that story about Alice in Wonderland . . . you remember? Alice shrinks down and the rabbit, or some such animal, is bigger than her . . .'

Edith sat down with her mug of tea in her hand intrigued by this strange line of argument.

'Yes, I remember.'

'Well, just imagine that happening to that lazy animal over there . . .'

The cat stretched and yawned widely as though Jackson's observations had reached its subconscious.

'. . . there you are! Just look at those wicked pointed teeth! If you were suddenly changed into the size of a mouse and hadn't the sense to hide in the back of the fireplace . . . you would be torn limb from limb. You could shout and beg for mercy as long as you liked . . . but would that vicious bloody cat . . . a first cousin to a tiger . . . show you any mercy? Now answer me that Edith.'

He sat back triumphantly, his case made.

'Come on then, I'm waiting for an answer. You tell me if that useless pet would have any conscience?'

Edith picked up the dirty dishes and made her way into the scullery ignoring the challenge. Five minutes later she returned indicating that she had lost interest in the argument.

'No answer eh?'

'Such an argument is so ridiculous it doesn't deserve a second thought. We aren't likely to be put in that position so you can forget about it.'

'I was talking about animal psychology Edith . . . getting inside the animal's mind. Them two horses will be trailing back to the hayfield this afternoon as though they haven't a scrap of energy left in their bones. Then at teatime, the minute they hear the milk cows bawling to come in for their cake, they'll have a new lease of life. Then when they get home they'll end up galloping down the paddock to reach the beck as soon as I take their halters off. I know animals Edith, the only person suffering from cruelty, is me . . . I will have to fight with them all afternoon if I expect to get a fair day's work out of them . . . I would only have to give in once and they would take the farm over.'

'Do you know, it's funny you should say a thing like that, because our Esther says a book has been written called *Animal Farm* where the animals take over the farm and the pigs rule the other animals . . . or some such rubbish . . . I don't know what these writers will think of next.'

'Exactly what I was just saying to you Mother, exactly the same thing! What's the writer's name? Is he from up here?'

'I've no idea.'

'Well you might notice such things when you hear

them. Fancy . . .' he mused to himself '. . . pigs taking over? . . . I wouldn't have thought they would have been the masters of the farmyard . . . the cats are a better bet . . . bloody ruthless they are . . . especially she-cats.'

Edith didn't like the turn of the conversation so she reached for something from the mantelpiece.

'Oh, I forgot to tell you . . . we had a postcard this morning from our May.'

'There we are, just talking about ruthless cats, no wonder you remembered about her card.'

'I wish you would say such unkind remarks to her face instead of me having to stick up for her in her absence.'

'She's too like that cat over there, she wouldn't take a scrap of notice of any advice I can give her. Anyhow, why has she sent us a postcard? She only lives in Egremont, she can catch a bus any day . . . unless she's been taken bad?'

His eyes gleamed at the prospect.

'If that's the case, she'll have to wait . . . we're too busy at haytime to do any sick visiting. Have you sent her a reply explaining that she'll have to ask your brother and his wife to look after her, they aren't busy with hay like we are?'

'No, she's not ill . . . God help her if she was, the way you talk about a helpless widow like her.'

'Why doesn't she get herself married again then, there must be at least one short-sighted chap somewhere in Egremont who fancies a clean house with a short walk to the town centre to crack with his friends.'

'She's on holiday.'

'On holiday! At a time when the rest of the family are busy haymaking? Where has she gone? London, to see that southerner of a son of hers?'

'Ambleside, she's spending a week with our Lizzie, she deserves a break Jackson, her life is a very lonely one. I wouldn't like to be left a widow like her.'

Jackson looked up in surprise.

'I've always thought that a life without me would be an ideal one for you Edith – no mucky clogs or early mornings.'

'No, I've got used to you . . . and they always say that the trouble-makers of this world are missed the most. You never tend to miss the nice quiet folks so much when they go!' she snapped as she swept her postcard from the dinner table.

'Well then, tell us what exciting things she's been up to in Ambleside, although . . .' he reflected '. . . she never sets foot in a pub where all the action takes place! There's nowt else to do in Ambleside that I can remember.'

'That's nothing to go by Jackson, I realise that the pub is the only place *you* can imagine being on a tourist route . . . there's some lovely walks near the lake . . .'

'She can come and walk around the hayfield here if she wants to go for a walk. I can't understand folks who have walking as a pastime . . . it's too much like work for me. Now a quiet sit in a pub listening to a good crack is worthwhile . . . and there's no effort involved. If she was like the rest of us working folks she wouldn't go traipsing along the edge of a lake like one of them lake poets I've heard our Jane say she was studying at one time. Lazy gentry! That's what she's trying to be if you ask me.'

'Well I'm not asking you. Ladies can't go and sit in a smelly pub wasting their money on beer and listening to a lot of men telling tales that they'll be ashamed to hear repeated the next day.'

She replaced the postcard on the mantelpiece, its shiny surface reflecting the morning sun.

'She says that she has met some very pleasant ladies in Lizzie's guest house who have travelled all the way from London by rail. All three have a lot in common.'

'No doubt she'll ask them if they know her son . . . or better still, she'll ask if they've met the Queen . . . after

42

all she'll only talk to them if they're in the same social bracket as herself.'

'Our May isn't as snobbish as you make out Jackson . . . we'll hear all about it when she comes home . . . and isn't it time you got away to the hayfield? I saw two of Tom's men go past a good hour since.'

'He needs to start them early, his men take their time about the work in the afternoons. It's only when you work for yourself that you have to keep up the pace all day. Hired men have to be chased along if you want to get a good day's work out of them. They're no better than the clydesdales that walk in front of them . . . always looking for an excuse to stop.'

*   *   *

'Such genteel ladies Edith!' murmured May as she settled at her sister's teatable a couple of weeks later.

'I'm sure they were May, and also I'm sure the break did you a lot of good.'

'Yes, our Elizabeth certainly took a step up in the world when she married Robert and opened that guest house. At first I thought she'd made the same mistake as you by marrying a man who works in a rough job . . . in the quarries, that is.'

Edith glanced at her sister, puzzled by the remark.

'What do you mean May? There's nothing wrong with working in the quarries, a lot of men in the Lakes work in the quarries, it's good pay in an area that's not got very much industry.'

'That's what makes it so enjoyable, there's no smoke and dirt, it's a real nice clean holiday area. Robert wears clogs for work, but he takes them off near the back door so that he doesn't offend the guests . . .'

Significantly, the sound of approaching clogs reached her ears. They crossed the yard and made their way

straight into the farm kitchen, much to May's disapproval.

She lowered her cup as if a nasty taste had found its way into the freshly brewed tea.

'Hello May,' greeted Jackson lowering himself into his favourite chair. '. . . it's nice to see you, it's a bit late for the haytiming and a bit early for the harvesting, so I reckon you've just timed it right.'

'Jackson means that we would have been out in the fields if you had come any other time. But as it is we have plenty of time to spare to hear how much you enjoyed your holiday in Ambleside.'

May nodded coolly, not altogether convinced about her brother-in-law's motives; greeting her so cheerily.

'Yes, I was just saying that our Elizabeth . . .'

'Who?'

Edith glared in her husband's direction as she passed him his usual mug of tea . . . his huge mug a pleasure he refused to relinquish even though the best china adorned the table in May's honour.

'Our Elizabeth,' repeated May firmly, '. . . lives a very comfortable life, in such a nice place. There were lots of visitors in the streets, I could hear lovely accents from all over the country . . . well spoken people, of course. You should take a holiday there Jackson, Bill is capable enough of running the farm now, Edith would love a week or so in the Lakes.'

Jackson looked startled.

'Our Edith and Esther spent a week up in Coniston last year trying out a three seater closet up at the Mines at our Sally's.'

'That visit had nothing to do with Sally's toilet May,' gasped Edith as she saw the look of unbelief and repulsion spread over her sister's face. 'Besides Jackson always exaggerates – it was a two seater.'

'How dreadful! Who would want to go to the toilet with someone else? I'm glad I was never persuaded to visit Sally. I very nearly did when Jim was lost in that blizzard when he fell down the mountainside into a snow drift after coming out of the quarry . . . I considered going to comfort her.'

'Just as well you didn't May, he didn't die . . . you can't comfort folks before they're dead.'

May ignored the implication of the remark and continued her account.

'As I was saying to Edith, I met two very pleasant ladies from London in *Elizabeth's* guest house . . .'

Edith's glance killed Jackson's questioning comment at its birth.

'They had very wisely chosen Ambleside for their holiday . . . they come every year by rail to Windermere . . . then take a taxi to Ambleside.'

'A taxi? What's wrong with the bus . . . or better still, why don't they stay at Windermere? It's so handy for the return journey?'

May lowered her cup and spoke deliberately and clearly to her brother-in-law as though he was hard of hearing or slow to understand.

'Win-der-mere?' she almost spelt the word, a heavy tone of disgust in her voice, '. . . it has a railway station, like Coniston . . . much too smelly and grimy for real ladies to stay. Ada and Connie were telling me that Wordsworth, the poet, prevented the railway from continuing on to Ambleside and Grasmere.'

'I've heard that he was a miserable old bugger.'

'Oh no, Jackson, there has to be places where the more sensitive people can enjoy the countryside without the interruption of noisy, dirty trains. I believe it's called *preservation*. Ada and Connie told me all about it as we walked to Rydal Mount.'

'I didn't know you went mountain climbing May?' observed an interested Jackson. Perhaps his sister-in-law had taken to the outdoors in earnest.

'Rydal Mount isn't a mountain Jackson. It's a lovely big house where the poet wrote a lot of his poems.'

'I thought he lived in Dove Cottage?'

'Oh yes, you're right Edith, he did at first, but you know he was the poet laureate in Queen Victoria's reign . . . naturally he couldn't be allowed to live in such a small place once he worked for the Queen.'

She nodded knowingly as she reached for another piece of cake.

'This is lovely cake Edith. It reminds me of the afternoon we three ladies spent in the café in the centre of Ambleside . . . you know the one Edith . . . four roads meet at that point. Ada, Connie and I sat at the table in the window, it was lovely, we could see all the visitors walking by.'

'Surely you didn't spend the whole afternoon eating a cream cake?'

'May was on holiday Jackson, you can sit as long as you like on holiday, it sounds lovely to me.'

Unease returned to Jackson.

'*You* had a good time last year when you went to Coniston, while *I* was left to manage the farm and to cook for Bill and me. I believe you found the time to go to Ambleside as well. Holidays like that cost both money and time on a busy farm. A walk to the beach at Nethertown would give you a good breath of fresh air if that's what you want Edith.'

'It's a change of conversation our Edith wants Jackson. I enjoyed talking about the Lake poets and local writers such as Hugh Walpole. It stimulates winter reading.'

'Winter reading! Our Edith never even finds time to read the *"Farmer's Weekly"* never mind a useless bit of poetry.'

'Now that's where you're wrong Jackson. At school I loved Wordsworth, especially *"We Are Seven"* and *"Lucy Gray"*.'

Edith's voice trembled as she thought of the sad

themes of the two poems. 'I always feel like weeping when I think of the words . . . we had to learn them by heart.'

Jackson was beginning to feel trapped in this holiday misery.

'Thank God I missed as much school as possible, I've never heard of anybody who went to Bookwell school crying over a sloppy bit of poetry. Whitehaven folk must have bloody awful taste in reading if you ask me.'

'Sensitivity! That's what it is Jackson. Ambleside, Rydal and Grasmere are very different from over here. This side of the county is much rougher, I'm seriously thinking of buying a house in Ambleside. I noticed one or two for sale.'

Jackson's face beamed at the thought.

'A good idea May. You could take in visitors. That would be nice.'

'Goodness me, no!' snapped May. 'A lady of means, no matter how little, doesn't take in paying guests . . . unless of course our Elizabeth was overbooked. A suitable lady guest might prove most acceptable.'

Jackson nodded thoughtfully. 'Very proper May. Men guests might be troublesome, especially if they visited the pubs in the evening.'

'Quite so Jackson. And it would be a nice place for Edith to come for a few days.'

'Edith would be no advert for your guest house May! She has too broad a Cumbrian accent . . . it would frighten other visitors away!' he observed gleefully as he rose to pick up his cap and make his way to the byre.

'I can't understand you marrying a man who is as ignorant as he is about the finer things in life Edith,' said May archly as she rose to get her coat.

'Well, May, he may have missed out on the finer points of poetry, but he's a manageable husband most of the time . . . and I always know that I can find him in the nearest pub . . . and not in another woman's bed like a few of those Lake poets,' snapped Edith as she accompanied her sister to the door.

5

A Good Move

'Jim Nolan has farmed on that farm for as long as I can remember, it'll be a bit odd to see a stranger working his fields.'

'Aye, so it will,' nodded Abe Mossop in Bill Brown's direction, then lowering his pint, '. . . he came here from Ireland a good few years back, no doubt you'll remember him coming Jackson?'

Jackson looked up from his game of dominoes and eyed his questioner speculatively.

'You'd think I was Methuselah the way you talk! Jim was farming here when I first came . . . a damned good farmer he was an' all. Irishmen rarely farm in this country so his ways were a bit new to us. I suppose they are only used to small farms with poor soil over there.'

'What about their horse breeding Jackson?' asked Alan Steel snidely, '. . . they can't be beaten for breeding and training racehorses. I'm surprised you've never taken a holiday over there to learn a few tips from the masters of the art!'

A chuckle went round the bar. Jackson picked up his hand of dominoes as though he had missed the challenge and slowly perused the options in his hand.

'It's a shame if a chap can't enjoy a quiet game of dominoes in his own local without being interrogated like a prisoner of war,' remarked Tom Graham, feeling that his friend was outmatched.

'Don't bother yourself about Alan,' snapped Jackson as he laid a doubtful double four on the table, '. . . a chap like me can't afford to go gallivanting around foreign countries to find out something that he learnt half a century ago here in our own area.'

Alan laughed out loud at the thought. 'Come on Jackson, how many Derby or national winners have you seen bred and trained up here in this remote corner of Britain? You'll be telling us next that none of us have noticed the pedigree animals grazing in our midst!'

The door of the pub opened as they waited to hear what the cornered farmer might reply.

A worried looking chap made for the bar, ordered a pint and then settled where he could watch the game of dominoes in progress.

'A nice evening.' Tom greeted the newcomer, '. . . I've never seen you in here before.'

'I was just taking a walk from Egremont, and folks say what a friendly pub this is, so I thought I'd drop in for an hour or so.'

'Well, Lad, everybody's welcome in here, maybe you'd like to tell us a bit about yourself . . .'

'Oh, no you don't get out of things as easily as that Jackson,' laughed Alan, '. . . I want to hear about the racehorse breeding here in this area, it's something that's new to me!'

'The trouble with you Alan is that you haven't travelled in your own district . . . if we sent you to Ireland, you'd not be able to tell them owt about where you come from . . . not like me who mixed with the gentry in the early part of this century.'

Pints were lowered in anticipation of this rare piece of news about Jackson's early life.

'Folks like you only think that everything worth knowing is learnt in school, but a knowledge of the history of this county is very enlightening.'

'For God's sake stop your rambling Jackson and let us all hear about the racing gentry,' urged Abe Mossop eagerly.

Jackson laid his last domino and moved himself to face his audience, ready to talk now that he'd lost his game.

'A pint wouldn't go amiss,' he announced as his clog pushed the sleeping Patch further under his seat.

Once settled he began his defence.

'The answer to your question is an easy one Alan – simply one name . . .' His listeners leaned forward, sure that the old man had for once been out-manoeuvred.

'. . . Hugh, the fifth Earl of Lonsdale . . . that's your answer gentlemen.'

'I didn't know that you mixed with folks like that Jackson,' laughed Alan in disdain.

'The yellow Earl . . .' continued Jackson as though no one had spoken. '. . . No Alan I've never met him . . . but I haven't met the Queen either, but I know all about her.'

He drew a long draught from his glass as he spoke. '. . . that's true education Alan . . . reading about what goes on in the world outside Whitehaven. I don't suppose any of you local folks would know what your own Earl got up to in the south of this country . . . or how he went to America and boxed against all-comers?'

Jackson was warming to his tale now, pleased to see the unbelieving looks on the faces of the listening farmers.

'. . . yes, lads! The yellow Earl showed the lot of them how we could fight in this part of the world.'

'But what about the racehorses?' asked Tom, now sure that his friend was on safe ground.

'. . . horses? horses? he was a friend of the king at that time . . . and you all know how expert the Royal Family is on racehorses! . . . the Yellow Earl was a keen horseman and raced his animals only with the best.'

He waved his arms expansively to illustrate his point. 'A Cumbrian like him would know far more about race horses than any Irish tinker . . . believe me.'

'I reckon you've earned a pint Jackson,' laughed Abe.

Alan interrupted the congratulations. 'I seem to remember you criticising the Earl of Lonsdale not so long ago Jackson, you reckoned that he had made his money out of the miners of Whitehaven ... remember he owned the coal pits and there was plenty of poverty and death there which he seemed to do very little about. I think we hear a different story according to what mood you're in Jackson.'

'There you go again Alan, you have very little understanding of how the gentry thinks.'

Alan laughed, '. . . come on then, enlighten us . . . we could do with a bit of upperclass thinking in the Grey Mare . . . our visitor will be impressed, I'm sure.'

The stranger nodded, obviously keen to follow the drift of the conversation.

'I've never met anyone who knows a lord,' he said.

'Neither have we,' snarled Alan, '. . . don't let Jackson persuade you that he has either . . . he can tell a good tale after a pint of Jean's beer.'

'Everybody knows that anything can be found out in good magazines and books.'

'Which magazines do you read Jackson?'

'There's one called the "Geographical Magazine" that our Jane buys for me every month . . . I can tell you Alan that it saves a curious chap a lot of money travelling around the world finding things out. Think of all the explorers who've died in African jungles and such like spots, when all they had to do was to buy a copy of the "Geographical Magazine" and you're taken right there without having to pack or suffer their terrible diseases. Yes, an education these magazines are . . . the trouble with folks like you is that you never stop to think that there might be an easier way of learning.'

'What has all that to do with Lord Lonsdale?'

'Well, Alan, that is where I read about his lordship and his racehorses, his boxing in America and his family life. Even though his family have lived in Cumberland for generations, the likes of us aren't going to find much out about him. It's only by reading these informative maga-zines that we learn about the gentry in our own district.'

'Well! I'll be blowed . . . I never thought you were so well read Jackson!'

'As for the poverty on his estates,' continued Jackson archly, '. . . all gentry in this country lived off slave labour . . . he was no different from the rest of them . . . after all, chaps like him were hammered with death duties.'

'I suppose you're right Jackson,' agreed Abe thought-fully, 'we can't expect our local Earl to be any different from the others.'

'That's right Abe, besides, some of the poor aren't worth bothering about . . . if you gave them a fortune they'd spend it the first week-end that they got it! By the way, does anybody know who's bought Jim's farm?'

'I've heard that it's a young chap whose father farms somewhere near Carlisle and he's buying him his first farm. I also heard that he's been studying farming in an agricultural college.'

'Good God, Abe, that's another well-managed farm about to go to the dogs!'

'Give the lad a chance Jackson, his father must be a successful farmer if he can afford to hand out farms right left and centre.'

'Any idea what his name is?'

'Paul Turnbull.'

'The second name is a fine one for a farmer, but Paul sounds a bit fancy. Anyway Abe, I'll wait to see how the lad does, maybe a few new notions might have us all looking over his gate.'

He turned his attention to the newcomer who had been listening closely to the conversation.

'And what do you make of all this then lad?'

'Oh, me? I've had a busy day at work in Egremont . . . things haven't gone so well, so I thought I'd take a run out here before I make my way back to Whitehaven where I live.'

Alan was interested. 'What do you do then for a living?'

'I work for the Gas Board, a salesman.'

'You shouldn't have any problems there Lad,' laughed Alan, 'the folk in Egremont have plenty of money ... can we offer any advice with your problem?'

'Aye, tell us all about it Lad,' encouraged Jackson.

'The trouble started last week when a woman came into the office to buy one of our gas cookers ... you know the offer ... £10 we give for your old cooker no matter what condition it's in, if you buy a new one.'

'Money to give away if you ask me!' snorted Jackson in disgust, '... no wonder trade is looking up in the shops in Egremont if the Gas Board gives spending money away like that.'

'Yes, it's a pretty good offer. As I was saying, this woman took up the offer, she lives in Lamb Lane, so we sent the fitters round with her new oven. They came back and said that they'd taken the old cooker to the Gas Board yard.'

'I can't see what trouble you've had with that, it seems like a good bargain for the woman.'

'Aye,' agreed Jackson, 'I know one or two folks who live down there, they know a bargain when they see one.'

The young man continued his tale.

'It wasn't the saleroom that made a mistake, it was the stupid chaps who fitted the oven.'

'What mistake?' asked an intrigued Abe.

'Well, only an hour or so after the oven had been fitted, the woman who bought it stormed into the office asking where her new oven was.'

'Now this is beginning to sound interesting,' observed Jackson gleefully, '... what had happened to her cooker?'

'The fitters hadn't looked carefully enough at the address . . . and you know that all the houses look the same in that part of the town.'

'But what about the woman who let them in? Why did she let them fix a new oven in her house?'

'The woman who ordered the oven said she'd be out and she'd leave the key under the doormat . . . we often get that sort of arrangement . . . both women must have left their keys under the doormat.'

'What happened next then?' asked Tom, '. . . the poor lass who bought the oven didn't have a new one at all!'

'That's right, she was furious. We told her that we must have delivered her oven to another house in Lamb Lane and we'd look into things. However, she'd no sooner gone than one of her neighbours came storming in to complain that she'd only gone down the street for some bread and some Gas Board men were seen carrying her cooker out of her house.'

'At least you got that bit sorted out,' laughed Alan.

'You might think we were on the home run, but you'd be wrong . . . the second woman had a chicken cooking in the oven, and our fitters had put it out into the Gas Board yard. She said her husband was due home from the pit and wouldn't take lightly to having no dinner ready . . . and what he would say when he spotted an expensive oven she hadn't ordered sitting in the kitchen, she daren't think about.'

The customers in the Grey Mare laughed in delight at the young man's dilemma.

'I thought all the excitement in the district took place out here,' chuckled Jean from behind the bar, '. . . what did you do to put things right?' she asked.

'We calmed the chicken woman down and persuaded her to keep the new oven, with a discount of course. She agreed, providing we went down to the Gas Board yard, found her chicken, as her husband might accept a new oven but not an empty plate when he got in . . . and all this before half past three, when she expected him home.'

'How did it all end then?' asked Jean.

'We searched through the discarded cookers, found the chicken, and returned it to its rightful owner. The first customer is to have her oven fitted next Friday, but we've insisted on her staying in, we can't offer ovens at give-away prices to everybody in the district.'

The stranger finished his drink as his tale drew to a close.

'I never seemed to have this sort of trouble in Whitehaven. It's because all the houses look alike in Egremont.'

'I wonder why you've come here to drown your sorrows!' laughed Jackson, 'I think you did very well to make two sales instead of one. You'll be named as salesman of the year if you ask me!'

'Unfortunately that's not the way the Gas Board sees things. In their eyes we all made too many mistakes, it was lucky for us it worked out so well. Anyway, I'm glad I called here, I can see the funny side of it all now.'

He rose to leave and thanked them for listening to his worries.

'That's the trouble with sending chaps from White-haven to work in Egremont,' laughed Jackson when the pub door closed, '. . . a local lad would have known which house it was without a second glance . . . and he would have smelt a chicken cooking in the oven. Whitehaven folks seem to lack a bit of ordinary common sense if you ask me.'

'I don't care where he was from Jackson, it was a damned good story, I'll have to tell our Mary that one when I get home!'

'I wouldn't boter if I were you Tom, she might just fancy ordering one of them cheap ovens, I'm not saying a word to our Edith . . . we haven't had the electric in very long and she might get the notion that gas is a better bet. No, tomorrow I'm going to offer to give Jim a hand to get all the stuff laid out for his farm sale. I can't go about buying cookers when I want to spend a pound or two buying a few things at Jim's sale, I've noticed he has a few in-calf heifers that would make a good buy, as well as some rather nice harness, some of mine is getting worn.'

'A good idea Jackson, I've noticed that your saddles are a bit worn and thin . . . I bet you've never bought a bit of brand new harness in your life.'

'You're right there Alan. Why should a thrifty farmer buy expensive harness when he can do a good neighbour a favour and buy what he's finished with – at least it won't need wearing in. And, he's not moving all his stock from one farm to another like I did a few years back. You farmer's sons have never known what it is to take stock, machinery and furniture miles across the county when you take on a better tenancy. We've moved twice and I can tell you it's a big worry. You should try driving cows and calves ten miles or more around the countryside, you wouldn't believe how many so-called farmers leave their field gates open!'

'It sounds like moving cattle in the Wild West!' laughed Alan, feeling smug that his father had left him a good working farm.

'Aye, well, it might be to somebody like you Alan, who's been handed everything on a plate. How would you like all the folks between here and Gosforth to see the sagging springs on your best sofa?'

'Don't you tell Edith what you've said in here,' warned an amused Jean, '. . . she'll deny having any furniture as bad as that.'

'Why do you think we were moving in the first place Jean, if it wasn't to have better land so that we could buy some better sofas and kitchen stuff.'

'I bet you bought all sorts Jackson!' suggested Alan mockingly.

'We would have made a profit here if it hadn't been for getting the electricity in ... it's been an on-going cost, sofas'll have to wait a bit.'

'Wait a bit? You've been on this farm for at least ten years, I feel sorry for your Edith!' laughed Jean.

'Well if she's not satisfied she should have married an iron-ore miner who lives in Lamb Lane with money and chickens to burn!' he retorted as he reached for his stick.

6

CONCRETING THE BYRE

'What on earth are you looking so pleased about Edith?' asked Jackson as his wife tore open a letter that had been delivered in the last five minutes. He was suspicious. Ordinary post which usually comprised bills and advertisements for seeds or cowcake, rarely brought such a look of pleasure to his wife's face. Surely it couldn't be from Aunt May again? He hoped not because her missives often heralded a visit which he felt unable to contemplate so hard on the heels of her last inspection! He automatically glanced at his fairly clean clogs, but no . . . Edith looked excited. Maybe they had come into some money? No, Edith would have looked worried. She had a naturally mistrustful mind about any good news of that sort.

'It's our Albert, he's coming home from Africa at last,' Edith smiled broadly and continued, '. . . you know that you've been saying that you would like that small byre concreted?'

'Aye, well, what about it?' asked Jackson uneasily.

'Our Albert is the very man to do it for you . . .'

Suddenly the door burst open and Esther made her way to the breakfast table.

'What man is going to do what? I hope you've decided to pay someone to mend the barn roof, there's a nasty piece of floor that looks as though it'll fall in onto the cows beneath if it soaks up any more rain water.'

'If folks would mind their own business instead of telling me to spend money on the landlord's property, this farm would be run a lot better. There's one of you wanting me to throw money away on somebody else's roof and the other wanting me to give her relatives a

61

handsome payment to concrete that bottom byre to house a few young heifers in a style that'll give them fancy ideas . . . I won't dare sell them to anybody in the district unless they have a byre with all mod cons. You know Esther, you can't trade successfully in this area if you have high-faluting ideas . . .'

'Don't talk daft Dad, it's time we tidied up our byres, farming is becoming a modern industry, and everything must be clean and hygienic.'

'Good God lass, have you never heard about good germs fighting the bad ones? If you make everything sterile and over-clean then you're asking for trouble. I blame that course you went on to at that agricultural College. You've never been sensible since that fortnight. God knows what such-like education is going to cost me . . . a poor struggling farmer.'

'You know as well as I do Jackson that the Ministry of Agriculture has been urging us to improve the quality of our buildings in order to raise the standard of public health and hygiene in this country.'

'Yes Dad, the government has decided that it's the farmers who are best able to educate the country in matters of health,' she added craftily.

Jackson nodded reflectively. 'Well, I can understand that well enough . . . I suppose they're not all completely daft in Westminster.'

'Who is the man you are asking to concrete the byre Dad? Anyone I know?'

'Your Uncle Albert,' announced her mother proudly.

'I hardly remember him . . . hasn't he been working in America or Australia?'

'No, Africa. But he did work in America before that.'

'Work? Work?!' laughed Jackson scornfully, '. . . he was one of those who went to the United States to find work when there was none here, then got sent back home for telling their bosses what to do!' Jackson chuckled gleefully as he settled to embellish his brother-in-law's past vices.

Esther laughed as she saw the twinkle appear in her father's eye at the same time noting her mother's unease.

'Skeletons in the family cupboard eh Dad? I'm in no hurry this morning I'd enjoy a trip down memory lane!'

'Take no notice of anything your father says Esther, you know how he can twist the truth when it suits him.'

'Oh yes, I know that, but *his* version will pass a hour or so on a Saturday morning before I go for my riding lesson.'

'That's another waste of time and money,' exploded Jackson, '. . . *my* lessons are free, but you don't seem to be interested. If you can stay on . . . then you can ride, that's all there is to it. You grow more like your mother's family every day with your fancy ideas about saddles and teaching horses how to jump. I've never heard of such a dangerous thing.'

'That's where I agree with you Jackson, it's much too dangerous for a young girl like her, she might be injured.'

'Who said anything about *Esther* getting hurt? The danger is when horses learn to jump over gates and dykes . . . there'll be no keeping them in . . . nothing but a bloody nuisance . . .'

'I'm waiting to hear about Uncle Albert.'

'Aye, well, he took off to America like I said to look for work. And he found it! But being Albert, he joined a Trades Union which were unlawful in the States in those days.'

'Disgraceful! Men should always be able to fight for their rights.'

'That wasn't the way the bosses saw it. They wanted value for money, none of this mamby-pambering that we have in this country.'

'He stood up for what he thought was only right and fair Jackson. It takes a man of principle to make a stand for the oppressed and downtrodden.'

'Oppressed and downtrodden?! Us working folks have always been oppressed and downtrodden no matter which country we live in, there's no need to leave home to fight a cause like that. No, Esther he should have known that as a foreigner in a new land like that he should have kept his mouth shut!'

'So what happened to him?'

'He left America . . .'

'You mean they threw him out Edith, along with the rest of the troublemakers.'

Esther chuckled at the thought of a brother of her mother and Aunt May being expelled from the United States. As if reading her thoughts Edith spoke quickly.

'Don't mention any of this to your Aunt May when she comes, she is rather sensitive about what happened.'

'You bet she is,' laughed Jackson, '. . . she always reckons that he was called after Prince Albert . . .'

'*She* would!' giggled Esther, 'I'm dying to meet this uncle, is he coming home soon?'

'Yes, he's spent a good number of years in South Africa working in the gold mines since he left America. The natives there needed training and assistance.'

Jackson chuckled louder at his wife's words.

'Work? He's not likely to work there either. All his trade union rules would be forgotten when there's so much slave labour available . . . and him not being the slave this time!'

Jackson was totally oblivious to his wife's suffering as he launched on his description of his absent brother-in-law. Esther, in spite of her awareness of her mother's misery, couldn't resist urging her father to continue his appraisal of her returning relative.

'Yes, Esther.' he continued gleefully. '. . . rights are for me . . . not for all men . . .'

'The natives were not ready for freedom Jackson, it's a slow process as you well know . . .'

'Oh aye,' agreed the old farmer, '. . . it's just like here in this country, we're supposed to be civilised, but the working man has few rights . . . just you try demanding your rights my girl. Oh no, the wisest thing is to bide your time and give a good day's work and you'll get a good day's pay.'

Esther smiled at her father's muddled philosophy, but decided not to pursue it too closely.

'Well then, what is all this about Uncle Albert and the byre?'

'I was just telling your father that I'm sure he would be only too pleased to concrete the byre for us, those heifers slip all over the place when the cobbles are wet. Besides, it's a disgrace that we keep any of our animals in such out-dated buildings.

'I think it's a good idea Mother, it would cost a lot of money to pay someone else . . . and I'm looking forward to meeting my long-lost uncle and hearing all about living in Africa.'

Jackson showed obvious irritation at the thought of his daughter consulting another member of the family about something beyond his experience.

'You only have to pick up a copy of the "Geographical Magazine" to find out what goes on throughout Africa. Real experts explore these far-away places carrying cameras and technical equipment to bring us the very latest information about what's going on out there. And, what's more, they spend their time *above* the ground looking at things, not down some dark gold mine full of black chaps slaving away and being cruelly treated by their lazy white masters.' He nodded knowledgeably in his daughter's direction.

* * *

A couple of weeks later, the cups clicked gently as Aunt May preened herself.

'You won't remember your uncle Albert, Esther?'

'No, Aunt May. He must have left home when I was small, but I'm looking forward to meeting him, I'm sure he will have lots to tell us about America and South Africa.'

'America!' snorted May in disgust. 'It was a waste of time him going over there. A young country with no traditions or monarchy! He felt completely alien to their brash modern way of life.'

'Yes May, he was an alien alright . . .'

'More rhubarb cake May? And this cream is very fresh.' Edith interrupted to steer the conversation into calmer waters. Esther's eyes avoided those of her delighted father.

'Civilised behaviour is unknown in those new countries Esther, Albert soon realised that the States weren't ready to accept expertise from Britain.'

'He went with the best of intentions May.'

'Yes, Edith, but retreat is often the best manoeuvre.'

'Definitely!' Agreed Jackson wickedly, 'especially if . . .'

'Jackson!' interrupted Edith sharply, 'weren't we discussing the possibility of him coming out here to concrete that byre now that the heifers are out grazing for the summer?'

'Concreting the byre? I'm not sure that he would have time to do a labourer's job. Remember he's been travelling on a liner for a number of weeks and will be used to resting on deck. He'll need a few weeks to acclimatise himself to this cold country. Besides, he'll want to spend some time with Ellen, she hasn't seen him for such a long time.'

'I'm sure it'll give him a place to escape May, wives can be very demanding, especially if he's made a lot of money.'

'That's another thing, he'll have no need to find work Jackson . . . although your kind offer was very thoughtful.'

'It was Edith's idea, I think that byre's good enough for any young stock we've got.'

Esther could see the prospect of meeting this interesting, much-travelled uncle receding into the distant future.

'I'm sure Aunt May agrees with me that in the interest of hygiene and mindful of the direct advice from the Ministry of Agriculture, Uncle Albert would be helping to make this one of the most modern farms in the district.'

May's gold earrings swung and twinkled their owner's ready acquiescence.

'Naturally Albert would be only too pleased to cooperate with the government. He must have met many important government officials on the liner coming home and will be well aware that Britain is leading the world at the moment in questions of world health and welfare.'

She smiled approvingly in her niece's direction.

'I never really approved of you going into farming Esther, but that course of study you did at Newton Rigg College has certainly opened your mind to the wider world, perhaps, in time, you may progress to administration in the world of agriculture.'

'Not a penny has she put in my pocket May since she went to that college. In fact I had to pay a few pounds I could ill afford to give her ideas that promise to take more money out of my pocket. Do you call that education?'

'Ignore his remarks May, he's really very proud of all Esther has done. Education is never wasted.'

'You're right Edith, but some folks can't see the way things are progressing since the war in this country, our Albert wishes to be in the forefront of progress. I'm going to see them tomorrow so I'll let him know that if he can spare the time you'd appreciate his advice on the modernising of your dairy facilities.'

'Please do that May,' smiled Edith.

Jackson did his best to control his rising temper, much to his daughter's amusement.

'You can tell him that I have a shovel just about his size if he wants to earn a pound or two by the sweat of his *own* brow for a change.'

Esther stifled her giggles while her mother began to fuss over her departing relative.

'How could three children of the same parents be so different?' she mused to her father as the door closed.

'Bloody busybody! Albert should have stayed in Africa and sent for May to come and bully his slaves into action. There would have been no need for extra brutality . . .

that sharp tongue and wicked eye would have kept their heads down . . .'

'At least she would have had a choice of *gold* earrings . . .' mused his daughter longingly.

* * *

'I see that you've been very busy the last few weeks Jackson, I hear that you've concreted that heifer byre . . . tarting the spot up a bit eh?' laughed Alan Steel provocatively.

'Aye, Alan's right, we're all surprised that you have money to throw about,' remarked Bill Brown casually.

Jackson glanced scornfully in their direction.

'The trouble with you chaps is that you never sit down and do any serious reading.'

'Serious reading? What sort of serious reading do *you* do then Jackson, I don't think you know where the nearest library is.'

'You're right there Bill, I've never set foot in a library in my life . . . never had the need . . . I get all my information from magazines. Now just take the "Farmer's Weekly", a grand magazine for a farmer who wants to keep abreast of the improvements in agriculture as well as the web of laws that surround our industry.'

'My God! You've certainly been educated since you last sat in here! "Agriculture" and "industry" in one sentence. Anyway, you seem to have put your hand in your pocket at last to make the sort of improvements that I made years ago.'

'I've noticed Alan that you jump on any bandwagon that comes along, but I've waited to see how things are going . . . and I think that this happens to be the right time.'

Alan chuckled.

'The right time seems to be when Edith's brother

comes home from Africa or somewhere and is available to concrete your byre free of charge.'

Jackson smiled tolerantly as he attacked a fresh pint.

'Now that sort of remark is no more than I expect from a chap who forks out money without considering how he can help someone else in the process.'

'What do you mean?'

'I mean that if you have a brother-in-law who needs a bit of a hand to settle back down in this country with a bit of extra money in his pocket while he is looking for a job, then that's the proper time to look for ways to improve both the farm and his pocket. I can't see anything wrong with that. Besides I have read some very interesting articles recently written on behalf of the Ministry of Agriculture which points out that hygienic standards should be observed if the health of the country is to be improved.'

'Thank God you don't go in for reading in libraries Jackson or we'd all be too ignorant to drink with you.'

'Libraries have nowt to do with intelligence . . . they're spots where folks go if they have a lot of time to fill in. But, any of you are welcome to call in any day and view my up-to-date byre. There's even a concrete trough built under the tap so that the heifers needn't go out in the snow and frost in wintertime, so if any of you are thinking of buying any of my heifers you can think again. I'll have to vet any possible buyers in case they lose condition under adverse management. I wouldn't like complaints to circulate about my stock being bought in first-class condition just to lose it in a matter of weeks, ignorant folks would think it was a fault in the breeding.'

Abe Mossop, who had been listening closely to the crack, nodded reflectively, then addressed Jackson.

'Can that foreign brother-in-law of yours build steps?'

'Not in my byre he didn't, clever as my cows are, they can't walk upstairs.'

Abe laughed. 'No, Jackson, the steps up to my corn loft need replacing.'

'You're right Abe, for the last ten years at threshing time, you've lost more good corn than enough as we've all tried to wheel the bogeys up there with the bloody steps sloping away from the barn wall, it's like trying to wheel a loaded wheel barrow along Striding Edge!'

'For once Alan's right,' muttered Jackson, '. . . I'll ask Albert to come round, maybe he'll be able to fix you up. My brother-in-law is available to up-date any farm buildings in the district, just hand your names in to me and I'll work out a work rota for you all.'

'Trust you to see that Africa's loss is your gain!' laughed Alan as he joined the game of dominoes.

7

HOPPELTY

'The price of eggs is bloody awful these days, I was wondering if there are any farms around here that sell eggs at the door,' queried the stranger, who wore a pair of very smart brown shoes, and leaned casually against the bar.

Jackson and his friends glanced up enquiringly from their game of dominoes in the 'Grey Mare'.

'I don't know what you townsfolk grumble about.' observed Jackson, glancing surreptitiously at his friends, his eyes twinkling at the thought of a clash of opinions in the offing.

'The likes of you, have no worries about breeding the hens, nor collecting and marketing the eggs. All *you* have to do is crack and fry them. I wish they reached our table as easily as that.'

'Oh, come on! You've grown your flock of hens for years – you probably can't remember when you last put your hand in your pocket to replace your stock. The ones I see when I walk past the farms are running around the yard feeding themselves. If you ask me . . .' the stranger continued challengingly, '. . . you farmers are always grumbling about something. You should be pleased when a customer is willing to come to your doorstep with good money in his hand.'

He turned again to Jean, and asked her to replenish his glass.

'The next thing,' snapped an irritated Alan Steel. '. . . you'll want our bacon, sausage, black pudding and milk . . . at the lowest possible prices!'

'What's wrong with that?' asked the persistent new-comer. 'I thought that's what you are in business for.'

'I wonder what gave you that idea,' interrupted Tom Graham, '. . . if we sold everything directly to the consumer what would happen to the small shops who rely on us for their trade? You know, there's more to farming than meets the eye.'

'Tom's right,' nodded Jackson. 'The casual observer can't possibly understand the trouble we have to produce a dozen good eggs simply by glancing over the farmyard wall then jumping to conclusions when they see a few well-behaved hens clucking around the yard. Often they're not the best layers.'

'What do you mean? Are the best layers locked up in the henhouse?'

'Be damned they're not,' snapped Jackson tetchily, '. . . the best layers are well out of sight, that is, out of everybody's sight. God knows where they lay their eggs. Our Edith often has a fair idea, but some can outwit even her.'

'I always thought that the farmer's wife locked her hens in at night to save them from being taken by foxes!'

Jackson nodded knowingly in his neighbour's direction, then continued with his explanation.

'Hens come in two sorts – just like humans do. Some never leave the safety of the farmyard and have to be looked after, then locked in every night. All too often these are the poor layers and if the farmer's wife is a bit careless about locking them in . . . then *they* are taken by the fox.'

'I would have thought that the ones that strayed would have been easy prey for the fox.'

'Now that's just where folks like you make a big mistake. The sort of hen, like our Hoppelty, can outwit any fox.'

'Hoppelty?' questioned the stranger with a laugh. 'Do you mean to tell me that you know your hens by name?'

'Jackson's stock lives for years . . . and years!' observed Alan Steel, by way of clarification. 'Any geese, ducks, hens or cows you might think of buying from him could be as tough as a rhinoceros!'

Jackson shuffled uneasily as a few titters could be heard circulating around the crowded bar. Quickly recovering his aplomb, he continued, '. . . but our eggs haven't shells like rhinoceros hide. Fresh as you can buy anywhere, you mark my words.'

'If the likes of your Hoppelty wanders the countryside, how do you know how old her eggs are then?' asked a puzzled Joe Watson.

'You shopkeepers are all the same – you think that every egg is laid with a lion stamped on it!'

The farmers chuckled, all of them aware of the new government rules regarding the age of eggs for sale in the shops.

'I never sell Hoppelty's eggs – because she makes sure that none of us see them. The crafty little bugger disappears every year for days on end, then hobbles homeward through the farm gate with a line of chicks obediently following her, as if to say, "I've outwitted the lot of you again!"'

'What's wrong with her if she limps?' asked the amused stranger, realising that he was entering unmapped territory.

'Probably has arthritis!' Joked Alan Steel, '. . . if Jackson's had her as long as I think he has, it's more than likely!'

The drinkers waited, anticipating the farmer's explanation . . . whatever it might be.

Jackson, undaunted by the question and Alan's cynical remarks, launched into a breezy explanation.

'Hoppelty is a mixture of white leghorn and a game breed . . . a real lively youngster she was. She has always been a grand clocker. We used to sit her on duck eggs, but she soon learnt that her offspring liked to swim in any puddle in the yard. The daft thing would dash round the edge of the water ordering her brood to come out and follow her. But, nature being what it is, they soon grew up and wandered off down the paddock to the beck with their foster mother frantically flapping behind them.'

'Did she limp then?' asked the intrigued visitor.

'No, the clever little hen bloody soon realised that we were hoodwinking her, so she took to laying her eggs as far from home as she could. She hatched many a clutch without us finding her. Then she paraded them through the yard as if to say "there you are! You can let the ducks hatch their own eggs, while I see to my own!" '

What about her limp Jackson? Did she have arthritis at that time then?' asked Alan grinning widely.

'Well, it was like this . . . one year we were mowing the far meadow, when there she was, sitting on a big clutch of eggs. We didn't see her until the last minute. But it was too late, the cutter had sliced clean through one leg as she dashed out. She'd built her nest right in the middle of the growing hay for safety, neither foxes, stoats nor rats had spotted her. Losing half a leg didn't seem to bother her, she was even more wily about laying away.'

'Why didn't Edith lock her in at nights?' asked Tom. 'Our Mary is always careful to shut them all in before she goes to bed.'

'A sensible idea Tom,' agreed Jackson, '. . . but Edith and Hoppelty seem to have an understanding. She says one good mother recognises another. The hen risks being killed in order to raise her own chicks instead of a pack of strange little swimming monsters.'

'What a lovely story,' sighed Jean from behind the bar. 'It's nice to hear of a bit of sentiment in farming.'

'Sentiment be damned!' snapped Alan tersely, '. . . the hen knows how to raise a large family without any help from the farmer's wife, and Edith is wise enough to realise it, so she lets the hen get on with it . . . I wish I had a few clockers as wise as Hoppelty.'

'Our Esther should have told them at agricultural college about Hoppelty, when she went on that course there. Instead she's landed home with all sorts of nonsense about buying new henhouses, then, believe it or not, scrubbing them out to keep them free from pests. Yes, she should have told them how ours breed out in the wild. I'm sure the old hen picks up no pests in the middle of the hayfield.'

'It can't be done like that Jackson,' laughed Tom, '. . . it would take all day looking for eggs.'

'That's right,' agreed Jackson, '. . . you chaps who pay only three shillings a dozen in Egremont Co-op get a bargain – our eggs are so labour-intensive that I wouldn't dream of selling you a dozen for under five shillings.'

'True enough,' added Abe sagely, '. . . the modern housewife wants . . . run-about, pest-free eggs these days . . . and, this is the right place to come lad. But nothing less than five shillings a dozen would guarantee you our prime quality eggs.'

The visitor shuffled uneasily.

'You farmers aren't so eager to make an easy sale as I thought you would be.'

He smiled resignedly as he spoke, '. . . anyway, I'll be making my way home. I'll say good-night to you gentlemen.'

'You saw him on his way Jackson,' said Alan after the pub door had closed behind the would-be customer, 'I thought you would have been only too eager to sell a dozen eggs or so at the gate?'

'Aye, well maybe, but I didn't like the way he made out that us farmers are a bunch of money grabbers – even if most of us are!'

The assembled company laughed.

'Besides, we don't want these slick townsfolk calling on our women when we're working our guts out driving a pair of sweating horses a couple of miles from home.

He can send his wife down the street to the Co-op like any other decent citizen.'

'Aye, the likes of him is far greedier than us,' agreed Tom, '. . . my Mary has enough to do while I'm out without gossiping in the back kitchen with a red-arsed miner.'

The farmers laughed at the popular reference to the iron-ore miners who worked beneath their fields. The game of dominoes progressed, but soon the companionable silence was broken by Joe Watson, the grocer, who began to chuckle to himself as he played.

'What's amusing you tonight?' asked Abe, irritated by silent thoughts.

'Talking about hens, I was reminded about when I was in the army in Italy. The peasants were very poor, but they were as generous as they could be to us.'

'Bloody fascists!' growled a voice from the long settle which flanked the far wall and was swathed in semi-darkness.

'The ordinary folk knew little of politics,' continued Joe, ignoring the comment, '. . . like us, they only wanted peace and an end to the fighting. But, like I was saying . . . we arrived at a small village in the hills and the villagers very generously gave us three chickens which they could ill afford to do. Now as always in every platoon, there's someone who knows how to kill and pluck a chicken. Sure enough a chap called Hiddleston volunteered to prepare the birds for the pot . . . and, by God we were hungry! The rest of us started to get everything ready.'

'Hiddleston must have been a farmer or a butcher.'

'He said he worked in an abattoir in civilian life.'

'You were lucky!'

'Yes, Abe, we thought so too. Well about half an hour later, he re-appeared with the three dead chickens, but they were awful roughly plucked!'

'A woman's job that,' nodded Tom, 'you should see

our geese when Mary has them finished ready for the table. But men don't have the time and patience to make a real skilful job.'

'Aye, well, we thought the same thing . . . and we were so hungry that a few feathers hanging on to the skin would be neither here nor there, so we set about boiling the water . . . it takes a bit of time when good dry wood is scarce. But it wasn't long before all was ready and Hiddleston went to fetch the hens he'd left in a cool spot under some trees . . . but believe it or not . . . he couldn't find them . . . not even one!'

'Had a dog eaten them, or the peasants sneaked back and taken them home?'

'No, although we searched high and low, we never set eyes on them, dead or alive. We reckoned they'd only been stunned and had come round then disappeared off back home!'

'A right sight they must have been,' laughed Abe, 'the Italians would welcome them back with open arms . . . *almost* ready for the oven!'

'Aye, lads, there's plenty of these townsfolk who reckon that they can do all sorts of things . . . but it's best taken with a pinch of salt. Maybe those Italian farmers breed a special breed with rubbery necks, we'll have to look into it!'

'Maybe you should write to the "Geographical Magazine" Jackson, it's just the sort of thing they like to investigate,' laughed Alan Steel as he laid his winning hand.

* * *

'You know, Edith, I think it would be a good idea to sell a few eggs at the door.' Announced Jackson cheerfully a few days later.

Edith turned in surprise. 'What on earth gave you that

idea? Don't you think I have enough to do without setting up shop on the roadside?'

'It would make a bit of ready cash . . . and maybe a dressed chicken or two . . . to provide an interest for you. You don't see many folks out here . . . it must be lonely at times.'

Edith glanced closely at her husband. 'I wonder who you've been talking to lately to make a statement like that. I've survived living on lonely farms for the past thirty years so I think I'll manage fine now without having to watch foodstuffs on the wall in case the dogs, cats and that stupid cow, Mollie, who can't keep her nose out of strange things, decides to eat the lot. I wouldn't be able to get on with my work for watching a basket of eggs and a few chickens losing their freshness on the farmyard wall.'

'You women don't think things out properly, you could write out a notice asking prospective buyers to call at the kitchen door . . . we'd make a few bob as handy as anything Edith.'

Edith still looked suspiciously in her husband's direction.

'Well, I'll think about it, the money might come in very handy for some new clothes. I've been fancying a trip to the shops, our Esther says older women dress very fashionably these days.'

Jackson could see the possibility of handy pocket money disappearing before his eyes, the conversation having taken a turn he hadn't envisaged.

'Maybe you're right,' he agreed philosophically, '. . . maybe it wouldn't be such a good idea. I wouldn't like to increase your work just for the sake of a few pence.'

Edith continued her work in a reflective frame of mind. Usually she could read into any innovative ideas Jackson might put forward, but today his logic was beyond her.

'He's getting a bit confused in his old age,' she thought to herself as she filled a bucket with corn for the impatient, cackling hens which waited eagerly for their morning feed.

8

EXPERTISE

The chinking of the swinging ploughing chains coupled with the crisp rhythmic ring of the horses' hooves on the tarmac were pleasant sounds to Jackson's ears as he and his two horses made their way home at the end of their working day.

He drew the animals to an unwilling halt as he reached a neighbour's field gate, then leant reflectively over the top rail to examine the newly ploughed land.

The two impatient horses didn't bother to graze the tempting grass along the hedgerows, eager only to reach their waiting feed. Captain shook his bridle in annoyance while the more patient Peggy rested one hind leg on the toe of her hoof.

'You can just stand there for a few minutes Captain while I weigh up the work this new chap's done today.'

A car slid slowly to a halt behind the two horses.

'Hello Tom! Travelling in luxury today I see.'

'Aye, well, I've just been to the auction to sell a couple of calves.'

'Did they sell out alright?'

'Yes, but as I expected I didn't get much for them, nobody wants to buy bull calves these days.'

'You're right Tom, if we could choose the sex of our stock farming would be too easy.'

He chuckled and turned back to the ploughed field, waving his hand briefly in the direction of the newly turned furrows.

'Even our new college-trained farmer can't place an order to the A.I. and end up with a succession of heifers.'

Tom had joined his friend and leant on their new

neighbour's gate. He nodded agreement, his eyes screwing up as his gaze appraised the recently ploughed land.

'Well, Jackson, Paul Turnbull doesn't own a horse so his work will be finished long before we're half way through ours.' He lit his pipe, then nodded sagely and continued his train of thought, '. . . that's the way things are going in the farming world now Jackson, whether we like it or not. A farmer'll hardly ever set foot on his land . . . he'll just ride over the top of it.'

Jackson nodded and gazed reflectively at the ultra-even furrows that striped the field.

'Jim Nolan spent many a long hour in this field sweating his guts out . . . and many's the time I've seen him sitting in that dyke-back drinking his tea and enjoying a few sandwiches. That mare he had, Blossom he called her, knew every bump and hollow in this field . . . she knew exactly when to start heaving into her collar to make it to the top of that nasty hump in the middle over there.' Jackson's tone was sad.

'Aye, well, maybe it's for the best Jackson, the old ways are going fast . . . look at them two horses of yours . . .' he indicated the restless rumps of the impatient beasts, '. . . it would take them a few days to plough this field . . . and I saw Paul start at about nine o'clock this morning and he shut this gate at around three. I reckon that's the way it should be done, not slaving from first light until you can barely see of a winter's afternoon. Us men and horses are only made of muscle and bone . . . younger farmers want a way of life without the pain and drudgery.'

Jackson glanced uneasily at his friend.

'Good God! What's got into you Tom? You sound like one of them wireless broadcasts for farmers. Them that you're usually too busy to listen to, unless it's a wet day. And like them experts you've overlooked one essential thing.'

'What's that then Jackson?'

'Money! I reckon if you have enough money to buy a couple of new tractors and the machinery to go with them . . . then you have sufficient brass to retire straight away and live the rest of your life in ease and luxury!'

Tom laughed. 'I thought my line of reasoning wouldn't appeal to you. In one way what you say is true, but from what I hear Paul has been set up on this farm by his father who has plenty of money. They say that money easily come by is easily lost, so it'll be interesting to see how he survives with only a college education to guide him.'

'I see he's had to widen this gateway to get his machinery into the field more easily,' observed Jackson, '. . . but I reckon he'll get bogged down as easy as Hell in the wet weather, it'll soon look like a building site, he really needs an entrance and an exit to every field if he's to beat the weather.'

He turned his attention to his two horses, who in unison, moved off in a homeward direction as soon as their master made the slightest move towards the farm. 'At least a tractor will wait a few minutes instead of reading a chap's thoughts and dashing off towards a full trough' he mused to himself.

Tom had climbed into his driving seat and sped off in the direction of both his tea and the milk cows he knew would be lined up at the meadow gate in response to the food trigger which was more accurate than any clock . . . except when the government in its wisdom introduced early summertime, then put the clocks back again in the autumn. At those times the cows were bamboozled for a few days, but they soon adapted to any change of routine which affected their feeding schedule.

Jackson's two horses plodded ahead leaving their master to reflect on the changes that farming had undergone during his lifetime and the likely changes which were to come.

'Ghosts,' thought the old farmer, '. . . these fields are

populated by the ghosts of farmers like Old Jim. Over the years, centuries even, the fields become old frinds, like mothers who feed us. Sometimes they tease and test the farmer as he learns how to manage the land and how to wrest good crops from the soil. Death,' he reflected, '. . . comes as a regular visitor to a farm – as does birth and renewal – there exists a sort of pact – if you treat me well, I'll reward you with a good living. Was college farming to be like that? Were there any short cuts to be learnt in an agricultural college? How would lessons in farming go? Doubtless there would be Chemistry like the chemistry set someone had given to Jane when she went to the Grammar School. But could love of the soil; the intangible message it gave as it trickled through your fingers . . . could that be set down as a formula and learned? The Chemistry set had seemed very like the Magic set she had received a year or so earlier . . . if you mix the right ingredients together you get a quick and satisfactory result. Through all his years of farming he had searched for a magic formula . . . but he had ended up depending on a mixture of good and bad luck along with a fair dose of kind weather. Would machinery and science give a good yield and make growth a certainty? Would desperate suicides become tragedies of the past? What would the ghosts of farmers past be thinking about all these changes as they watched over their beloved fields?'

Jackson shook himself back into the present as he entered his farmyard and headed for the water trough where his almost redundant animals were drinking the water faster than Alan Steel could down a pint on a thirsty Sunday night. 'Come on you two, let's get you unharnessed and fed before them cows bawl their hungry heads off.'

* * *

'I see there's a ploughing competition at Pickett Howe Farm, Egremont at the beginning of September,' observed Bill, the 'Whitehaven News' in his hand.

His father looked up enquiringly from his plate of steak and kidney pie.

'What are you telling me that for lad? It's a good number of years since I was daft enough to enter any of them competitions. Mind you, I've won one or two, but it's a lot of bother. I would have to spend time and energy practising and training them two daft horses how to keep their noses straight instead of staggering along the furrows like they usually do.'

'I wasn't thinking of *you* entering the competition Dad.'

'Then who else can you think of on this farm that might have a go?' asked Jackson dismissively.

'Why, *me* of course!'

'*You?* Good God! you know fine well that I have to send our Jane to start harrowing every field you plough, before you get half way through the job in case any of the neighbours pass by and see the grass still sticking through ... and spot the wavy furrows that look as if you've dosed the horses with a couple of bottles of beer each before you started.'

Bill's face hardly changed, he was used to his father's poor opinion of his expertise with a plough. He waited patiently for the end of the assessment then pursued his objective more shrewdly.

'But, maybe you could coach me a bit, John Mossop has entered already and I thought it was time that I had a go. John has won it for the last two years, so I reckon he's had enough good luck.'

Jackson's attitude changed immediately he heard that a neighbour's son had done so well over the last few years.

'Maybe I've been a bit too hasty lad, a bit of expert coaching could work wonders.'

'I think it's a daft idea,' snapped Edith.

'Oh, and what reason have you for saying such a thing?' asked her husband.

'Just stop to think for a minute, as well as being a decent ploughman, you have to deck the horses out in fancy gear . . . and we don't possess anything smart and eye-catching which might win a prize. Leave all that for the experts who have entered these competitions for generations and have the correct tackle.'

'Well, how's that for a defeatist attitude! If we'd had to rely on an attitude like that during the war we'd all be goose stepping and saluting Hitler by now.'

'That's right Dad, we'd have the "Whitehaven News" printed in German . . .'

'There's no talking sense to the likes of you two . . .'

'You know Bill, if you go and look in that little harness room above the hay barn, you'll see some ploughing brasses and fancy bits and pieces that Mother can polish up for us . . . they'll look fine. But it's the ploughing that matters. Never bother yourself lad we'll show them all the way to plough a field before the month's out.'

'I'll not polish any rotting ploughing harness to please anybody. In any case, I wouldn't do it right and you'd be saying that I lost you the first prize . . . for once you can both do your own dirty work.'

Edith flounced out of the kitchen.

'There you go! A chap asks for a bit of help and that's what he gets! No co-operation at all . . . a chap has to do every hand's turn for himself . . . but, at least I'll know that it's done properly . . . dressing the draught of horses is a skilled part of the competition. First thing in the morning we'll start on the six acre and train Captain and Peggy in the ways of ploughing matches.'

'I think women should be allowed to enter the competition,' announced Jane who had been listening to the animated conversation.

Her father glanced at her in horror. 'Don't you think I have enough of a problem on my hands teaching our Bill and two strong-willed horses without struggling to get a lass to find her way from one end of a field to the other without tripping over a stubborn cobble or being buried in a sandy furrow.'

Jane flounced out of the kitchen in the wake of her mother muttering about the narrow-mindness of the male sex in general.

'Take no notice of them lad, they're like all she-animals . . . forever wanting to do things that they were never intended to cope with. Why they can't be satisfied with sitting in the house watching the rain dripping down the window while they're nice and warm . . . and switching the electricity on and off now and again, I can't imagine. God made them to live a comfortable life . . . but they choose to spend their time getting in the way of folks that do all the hard work.'

EXPERTISE

* * *

'You must hold the handles level Bill and tighten the cords a bit more, if you tangle them up like that next week the judges'll think you've spent last back-end knitting that winter sweater you're still wearing.'

An exasperated Bill swung the plough round as he reached his irate instructor who was coaching comfortably placed in the gateway. He was beginning to regret his decision to enter the competition along with his mates. A bit of bravado in the Young Farmer's Club had resulted in a verbal grilling from his father that was on a par with that handed out by the gestapo.

One or two passers-by had stopped at the gate to witness all the unusual activity in Jackson's field.

'I reckon Bill stands as good a chance as anyone,' observed Alan Steel from his perch on his Clydesdale mare.

'No chance at all, you should see John Mossop's straight furrows . . . you'd think his plough had some sort of mechanical clock on it that controlled the evenness of the ploughing . . . expert work I call it.'

Jackson was within earshot of his 'friends' remarks.

'Let's see a bigger effort lad, keep them two buggers facing in the right direction, you're letting them wave their heads about like two hungry stoats. They can't plough straight if they're not looking straight in front.

'It's the first time in my life that I've felt sorry for Bill Strong,' said Alan quietly to the other observers.

'Don't you feel sorry for him Alan, he's never known anything else . . . and the old man can be very generous when it suits him.'

Alan laughed at Tom's remark. 'I've never thought of Jackson as being a kind father . . . he treats his family worse than he treats the stock . . . he sees his family as an on-going cost, whereas the stock turn themselves into money. But, just look at the improvement in that last furrow! Bullying seems to work after all!'

'That's better,' yelled Jackson as the team neared the waiting spectators. Peggy shook her bridle in exasperation, annoyed at the slow pace of things ... for her, every time she managed to raise her head the dyke seemed to be further away.

'You can stop your rattling about and watch where you put your feet milady. You've had far too much of your own way in recent years, it's time you had a bit of retraining,' snapped Jackson reading the mare's thoughts.

'She's too old to get over the shock of a retraining programme Jackson ... and next week when you want the job finished on time, she'll dawdle about like a love-sick lad.'

Jackson raised his gaze to the watching neighbours.

'What a pity you chaps have nothing better to do than spy on a hard working neighbour ... you'll make my horses think they're in a bloody circus ring.'

'Why don't you blindfold them then Jackson? that way they'd manage the ploughing match fine ... that is, if they're so damned temperamental!'

'I reckon it's the judges that'll need to be blindfolded Alan,' laughed Bill Brown.

'You can stop now Bill,' snarled Jackson, '... a chap can't be expected to concentrate when half the countryside has turned out to watch a field being ploughed, you'd think the Picture House had shut down in Egremont and they were short of a bit of cheap entertainment.'

* * *

'What a pity neither of us had time to go to the ploughing match this afternoon,' observed Jane as they prepared the tea table for the return of the men. 'I spent hours cleaning up those horse brasses, I didn't know we had any.'

'They were in a small harness room when we came here, you never know what you find in the far corners of a farm when you take over.'

'Well, I can understand why they left them behind, my finger nails will never be the same.'

'Say nothing to your dad about broken finger nails, he thinks clean hands are a sign of idleness . . . just keep your thoughts to yourself.'

'I'm well aware of that Mam, but after all my polishing I hope they might have won a small prize.'

She glanced out of the window as she spoke. 'Here they are . . . the horses look lovely, I think I'll take a photo of them, otherwise nobody will ever believe that our horses could look so splendid!'

Jane dashed outside passing her father on his way in.

'How did Bill come on then Jackson?' asked Edith eagerly.

'Will you let a chap sit down before you interrogate him, I've stood for hours watching draughts of horses crawling up and down a sticky field.'

Edith busied herself serving the ham and eggs, aware that things had not gone exactly as had been hoped.

Two minutes later a tired Bill took his place at the table.

'That ham smells lovely,' he observed hungrily.

'Bill didn't win,' said Jane sadly as she took her place, '. . . I hope the brasses didn't lose points for him.'

'No, the ploughing competition was won by the best example of ploughing that was there,' sighed Jackson.

'Well, who won?' asked an exasperated Edith.

'Paul Turnbull,' replied Bill as he tucked into his tea.

'Paul Turnbull?' repeated Edith, '. . . I thought he didn't keep any horses.'

'There were no conditions about who owned the teams,' snapped Jackson, '. . . apparently Paul borrowed a couple of very fine Clysdesdales from a cousin near Cockermouth and has been practising most afternoons after work.'

He nodded his head thoughtfully, '. . . there is something to be said for letting the tractors do the heavy work and saving a chap time for a decent hobby.'

Bill and Jane glanced at each other. Perhaps their father would decide to buy a new, much wanted tractor after all.

Jackson lowered his mug as they waited expectantly for his next thought.

'But the trouble with that is I couldn't keep a couple of idle horses eating their heads off and laughing over the dyke while I struggle to keep warm on top of a stinking, noisy piece of tin. No, I reckon I'll let things move along as they are . . . I know that *I'm* in charge of things as they are.'

The two children nodded knowingly at each other . . . they were, sadly, only too aware that their father *was* 'in charge'.

9

MILK

'I'm sorry to hear that your young neighbour's confinement was so difficult and took so long,' said Edith sympathetically as her sister paused in her account to reach for yet another cream cake.

May nodded. 'It was the fact that it was twins that caused most of the problems. You know these modern hospital qualified midwives seem to spend so much time sticking needles and anaesthetics into the poor patient, that things are slowed down a lot.'

She lowered her voice discreetly, glancing in the direction of her brother-in-law who had taken refuge behind the startled pages of his favourite farming magazine.

'I've always felt,' she continued confidentially, '. . . that a good scream eases things . . . it's nature's way you know . . .'

Edith shook her head sharply in disagreement. 'How can you allow a lass to suffer when there's help for her May, it's alright saying these things until the day it happens to you.'

'No, the Bible says a woman "travaillest", that means that she's expected to suffer pain because of the sinful way she has lived.'

Jackson lowered his magazine, his interest aroused by this theological insight.

'What sin May? It takes two to sin if you're talking about getting kids. I've never heard of a woman going it alone . . . so to speak.'

May's earrrings flashed angrily in the firelight as they swung in Edith's direction.

'Just listen to that crude speech Edith . . . real gentle-

men are too discreet to mention the coarser side of life.'

Jackson raised his magazine abruptly, muttering that he had never met a 'real gentleman' in his life let alone laid any claim to being one.

'Two babies need an awful lot of attention,' continued Edith in an attempt to divert any verbal storm.

'Feeding them is the big problem at the moment,' continued May, '. . . the girl hasn't enough . . . ' here she lowered her tone an octave . . .

'Milk!' snapped Jackson.

A startled May rattled her cup angrily. 'This is women's talk, we don't expect men to understand any of it . . . the suffering of a young mother is too sensitive an area for rough men.'

Milk

'How can you say a thing like that to a dairy farmer? We're experts on that sort of thing . . . milk yield, like the sort of cream you've just enjoyed, is the result of selected breeding and careful feeding. I notice that the doctors don't seem to hand out feeding programmes to their expectant mothers. If they want their patients to have easy deliveries and a fine milk yield they have to feed and plan for it.'

'Come! come! Jackson! You can't compare a woman with a cow . . . a common animal led by instinct.'

'Can't I! Well, May, instinct put the lass in the condition she was in in the first place . . . and . . . I haven't noticed the birth rate going down. In fact I read a lot about these new birth pills . . . so instinct and nature seems to have the upper hand if you ask me.'

'But two babies need a lot of milk as you know May, she'll have to put them on the bottle, I can see no disadvantage in that . . . her husband, or her mother can help to feed the twins then.'

'Yes, you're right Edith, there are plenty of folks in the family who will be willing to help her I'm sure of that . . . but she should be sure to buy some of those birth pills that Jackson mentioned if she's to recover completely from such a difficult confinement and build up her health again.'

Jackson lowered his magazine and spoke reflectively.

'You mention a mother having two babies to look after and feed. Well May, have you ever heard of a foal with two mothers?'

'How ridiculous! Nobody can have two mothers, not even one of *your* foals.'

'Well now, let me tell you a true story.'

May settled herself with a fresh cup of tea and waited for her brother-in-law to spin his yarn, a look of disbelieving disdain on her face.

'Edith,' he addressed his wife, 'You'll remember that

Clydesdale mare we once had called Lady? It was years ago when we farmed at Coulderton.'

Edith thought back. 'Oh, yes,' she recalled after a moment's reflection. 'I remember her very well, she had a very friendly disposition.'

'. . . aye, well, that might well have been. But she was one of those mares that didn't like dropping her foal if anyone was watching her.'

'That's a silly remark for a start,' snapped May '. . . foals must be like babies and come when *they* see fit . . . some women have their babies in surprising places, like taxis, lifts and waiting rooms . . . you can't tell me that they wouldn't have waited if they could have done. This is just one more of your outlandish tales if you ask me.'

'I don't know as much about human deliveries as you do May, but I reckon I know a damned sight more about mares and foals. So if you'll just sit and listen quietly you'll learn a few true facts that you can entertain the ladies with at the Mothers' Union.'

May sipped her tea, a pained expression stealing across her face. 'Talk as long as you like Jackson, but you can't persuade me that a foal can have two mothers.'

Unperturbed by the scepticism of his listener Jackson continued his story.

'Like I said, Lady wouldn't foal if she thought she was being watched, so she usually foaled during the night. I remember she was in a field with a herd of milk cows at the time.'

He turned in his wife's direction. 'You'll remember Edith, we had a cow at that time called Paddy, she had horns that curled evenly round her head like a crown.'

Edith nodded. 'Yes, we had that cow for years, she was a rather pretty roan.'

'You'd think your cows lived for a hundred years the way you remember each one of them,' snapped May, still suspicious of the verity of the tale.

96

'We've had to May, we couldn't afford to buy new ones if they didn't give plenty of milk, like this new mother you're talking about . . . inferior breeding if you ask me.'

A look of disgust replaced the scepticism on May's face.

'Go on with your story,' urged an uneasy Edith, 'May will have to leave to catch the bus before too long.'

'I have plenty of time to finish the story. Like I was telling you, the mare must have foaled in the dark somewhere near to Paddy and both she and the cow had licked the new foal.'

'How on earth could you know what had happened in the dark when you were nowhere near?' asked a triumphant May.

'You can believe it or not just as you will May . . . but from the day of its birth that foal fed from both the mare and the cow . . . what a fine healthy animal it was . . . a mixture of mare's milk and cow's milk made it grow faster than any foal we have bred before or since.'

'That's all perfectly true May. It was at a time when you were living down south or you would have seen it for yourself.'

May wrinkled her nose in disgust. 'You would never catch me spending my time looking at animals with unnatural habits. I'm not really a country person.'

'No, I reckon you're not,' observed Jackson, '. . . but you must remember that the Queen owns at least one farm and breeds a lot of horses, so it's a good idea to know something about their habits. I mean, just supposing you were invited to Buckingham Palace and you had no idea what to say to members of the royal family, you could tell their Majesties about the foal with two mothers.'

Edith laughed at the thought. 'Tell May about the cow coming back home to be with the foal Jackson, it was all true.'

'Well, as you probably know May, licking creates a bond between the mother and the foal . . . and both Lady and Paddy thought that the little foal belonged to her. The foal, knowing no better accepted that he had two mothers to feed him . . . I mean no young animal in its right mind would turn down the offer of an extra milk bar. So, when I took the mare to work in the fields for the day, the foal, Prince we called him, didn't follow his mother out of the field like the other foals did, he just stayed behind with his other mother and was fed and cared for in the field until his real mother came home. Other foals were shut in a hull where they would be safe until their mother came back from work. I couldn't leave a motherless foal to wander about in the field alone.'

'This story is unbelievable,' said May uncertainly.

'That wasn't all the story either,' continued Jackson as his erstwhile antagonist listened in spite of her doubtfulness. Jackson continued his account, '. . . we used to have a couple of grazing fields which we rented from Marlborough Farm, that big farm between Coulderton and Bigrigg. We took the cows along there first thing in the morning after they'd been milked to graze for the day. Well, after Prince was born, Paddy would be driven with the rest of the herd down the road to the Marlborough fields. But often, by the time we had driven the herd into the field then fastened the gate, that bloody Paddy, who had led the lot of them all the way and gone in through the open gate, had found her way out, over the dyke and had dashed back home to be with her foal – Prince. Sometimes she reached the paddock before we did . . . other times she was a bit late, but there was no way we could part her from her baby.'

'It all takes a lot of believing,' announced May looking earnestly at her sister, unsure whether her brother-in-law was spinning one more of his tall tales. But Edith was nodding in assent. 'People say that animals have no finer feelings May, but that cow loved another mother's

offspring with the devotion that is sometimes missing in the human world.'

'How did she get out of the field Jackson, why didn't you repair the dykes?'

'When a woman is determined enough, as you well know May, she can overcome any obstacles . . . Paddy always managed to climb over . . . and besides, it wasn't our own land . . . it was parcel land that we hired for extra grazing. I couldn't ask the owner to repair his dykes because we had a lovesick cow that was convinced that a foal was her calf . . . could I?'

'A strange story Jackson, it's hardly believable.'

'They say that fact is stranger than fiction,' mused Edith, grateful that for once her husband and sister were holding a civilised conversation without any acrimony.

Jackson stood up and reached for his walking stick then glanced at the clock.

'The cows will be waiting to be milked. Not one of them have calved out dry . . . no the medical profession has a lot to learn from us farmers May. But none of them will admit to being short on breeding knowledge . . . maybe the old idea of a wet nurse, like the queens and rich ladies used to have for their babies, might be a good idea. Rich women didn't like the thought of feeding their own babies with their own milk, never mind a hungry little stranger like Prince.'

'I never thought Jackson was capable of such sensitive feelings,' observed May thoughtfully.

'You should never judge people by their rough exterior,' agreed her sister, pleased at the outcome of this visit.

The kitchen door re-opened and Jackson leant inside for a moment.

'And that foal, as a yearling won second prize at Carlisle auction . . . just think of that May! Just because it couldn't tell its mother's tits from anybody elses!'

The old farmer's chuckles could be heard echoing

through the scullery as his sister-in-law donned her hat and coat the look of disgust taking its rightful place on her face.

'Your Jackson spoils himself with his crudeness Edith, I don't know why I believe a word he says, it all sounds very far-fetched . . . whoever heard of a foal having two mothers?'

10

PASSING ON

'**M**y goodness Dad you do look very smart this morning. Can I help you to fasten that tie? You can't be used to dressing up like this!'

'That's enough cheek from you my lass, you'd think I never wear a suit.'

'You never do.'

'Your father's going to old Peter Garret's funeral this morning and Tom will be calling for him soon so don't hold him back.'

Jackson laughed, 'I don't know what you're fussing for Mother, Peter's not in any big hurry!'

Edith brushed his jacket impatiently.

'You'll manage to get there when it's all over and folks will say that you didn't pay your last respects to a good friend of many years standing . . . quite truthfully they'll think you're only interested in drinking to his memory in the "King's Arms".'

'Well, I can't think of a better thing to do. I hope when folks come to my funeral they'll have a drink and a good laugh, because if I'm hovering above I want to hear a good crack, not miserable tales of woe . . . which probably aren't true. If everybody's having a good laugh I'll know that the truth is being told not a load of hypocrisy!'

'Don't you dare walk into the church late, or I'll be ashamed when I go to the Mothers' Union if Mrs Shepherd and the others have any bits of scandal to relate.'

'Mrs Shepherd is a sanctimonious gossip-monger, nobody takes any notice of her Mam,' added Esther.

'People repeat what these gossips say even though

102

they know they are only half truths. But your father needn't give cause for idle chat, he can just get himself into the church in good time and make sure that Tom arrives early as well.'

'I never know why we have to sit through a lengthy funeral service anyway, the chap's already arrived in either Heaven or Hell at least three days ago, so I reckon the vicar's remarks are a bit late.'

'It's a question of paying our respects and thanking God for giving us the life of Peter Garret,' explained Edith sharply.

Jackson looked in surprise at his wife. 'I thought it was his parents who gave him life?'

Esther giggled.

'Just you get along to that church and keep your heathen thoughts to yourself, the vicar knows what he's doing without any advice or embellishments from you.'

'I'll be the soul of discretion Edith as always when faced with mysteries that are beyond the understanding of a simple farmer . . . and stock breeder . . . ah here is Tom . . . I should be back about teatime to milk. But in case I'm a bit late you can start without me Esther . . . and don't forget to water the bull.'

The master of the house hurried out to the waiting car leaving an anxious Edith and an exasperated Esther in his wake.

'That means that I'll have to do the milking by myself . . . and he knows how I hate watering the bull . . . and what's more, the bull knows that I'm a bit nervous of him. Some modern farmers have had water put into all their byres, but not Jackson Strong, it would be too much like a convenience.'

'Your father does what he thinks is best Esther, I'm sure the bull is harmless, otherwise he wouldn't expect you to lead it out to the trough in the yard. Maybe it needs exercise.'

'Exercise? If it tossed me it would have great exercise

and a lot of fun! What I usually do is to carry buckets of water into its stall, it drinks gallons but that's better than leading it across the yard. But don't tell dad that I do it that way or he'd blow his top.'

'Don't worry, just you get on with the work, what he doesn't see won't bother him.'

'He has a way of knowing what happens when he's not there, you'd think he could talk to the stock!'

'Well, we all have to make sacrifices from time to time, a person only dies once and it's important that the neighbours pay their respects in the timeless manner.'

'The timeless manner is spent in the "King's Arms", the funeral is at half past eleven and milking doesn't start until four o'clock. I can't see the local farmers spending that length of time praying for the soul of Peter Garret.'

* * *

'It was a grand funeral,' observed Alan Steel as he settled to his pint, '. . . we certainly know how to give a chap a proper "send off" in these parts. And luckily it managed to stay fine all afternoon.'

'I wonder how any of you notice the weather in the afternoon, seeing you would spend most of it in the King's Arms or one of the other pubs in the main street.'

'Now then Jean, just because we weren't spending a few of our hard-earned shillings in the Grey Mare . . .'

'It doesn't matter to me where you were, I only know that none of you would be out braving the elements as long as a pub door was open.'

'Don't we spend most of our lives *braving the elements*?' exploded Jackson, '. . . and this pub reaps the benefit!'

'That's right,' nodded Alan Steel in agreement. 'These pubs in the countryside, in the middle of nowhere, can only flourish because us farmers patronise them.'

'So just mind your manners young lady or we'll take our custom elsewhere.'

'I'm not worried Jackson, I know that you can all manage to stagger home from here, but you'd have a job to stagger all the way from Egremont . . . a bit more politeness and consideration wouldn't go amiss in this bar.'

'Now she's going all hoity-toity on us,' laughed Tom, '. . . you'd think she'd be pleased that we've paid our respects to an old friend in the best way possible.'

'Today's peaceful funeral reminds me of the coffins we sometimes had to carry on board ship.'

The speaker was an elderly man who had been listening closely the account of the funeral.

'Aye, I forgot you were a seaman Jock,' Alan Steel remarked, '. . . I'm sure you must have some strange stories to tell. Why did you have coffins on board anyway?'

Jock smiled as he remembered his seafaring days.

'We used to sail from Liverpool to South America and then back home and I can tell you that we collected some strange cargoes. The funeral reminded me of the coffins we used to bring from Brazil back to Portugal. The older Portuguese had left the old country at the beginning of the century to look for work, and hopefully, wealth in Brazil which was a Portuguese colony. Many of them had made vast amounts of money over there, but when it came to the end of their lives they wanted to be buried in the old country . . . so their bodies were sent back by cargo ship. Of course the sailors knew that very often the coffin was packed with money and expensive jewellery for the family back home.'

'They would be dodging the import tax I suppose,' agreed Alan.

'Yes, that was the idea, but the Portuguese didn't reckon with our foreign crew . . . the ordinary seamen can smell money no matter how far down it might be buried in the hold.'

'How disgraceful!' said Jean.

'So it was,' agreed Jock, '. . . but the world is a rough place and they knew that the family was trying to cheat the authorities anyway.'

'What did they do?' asked Abe Mossop eagerly.

'You can well ask,' laughed Jock, '. . . they did what they usually did . . . they waited until us officers were busy . . . on watch . . . or eating . . . and then they went down to the hold with a screwdriver and opened the coffin lid. They were experts at finding the loot which was hidden about the corpse.'

'Didn't the body stink?' asked an intrigued Jean.

'Aye, that's an interesting point,' observed Alan, '. . . I wouldn't fancy poking about a dead body.'

'No, the Doms, as they called the wealthy Portuguese, had enough money to have the bodies embalmed . . . but I don't think a bit of a smell would put some of them sailors off taking the money.'

'It would have served them right if they had caught some disease from the bodies, I should think some terrible tropical germ might have killed the person in the first place! There doesn't seem to be any justice in this world.'

'But Jean, you must realise that them folks had been impoverished and had emigrated to Brazil with nothing in their pockets . . . then plundered the natives to make themselves rich . . . I reckon they deserved to have it taken from them.'

'What! Just to have it spent on drink in Liverpool?'

'Now there you are jumping to conclusions, sailors were badly paid and often badly fed on them ships, they had families to feed at home too . . . a bit extra cash came in handy.'

'That's very interesting,' remarked Jackson, '. . . we hear a lot about hungry farms, but the same must have been true of the shipping lines, eh Jock?'

Jock was pleased to have such an interested audience.

'Yes,' he agreed, '. . . we all knew which lines were the

hungry ones . . . though one shipping line was very good and paid part of the men's wages directly to the wives because the owner, who was a woman, knew that many of the sailors drank their money as soon as they were paid on the dockside, so very often, it never reached the wife and family.'

'I can't understand why some men starve their own children,' remarked Jean tartly.

'That was very common in the early years of this century,' replied Jock, '. . . but sailors weren't the only ones who were guilty, I'm sure of that.'

The assembled drinkers nodded in assent.

'It was always common around here,' said Tom, '. . . but we tend to think that places like Liverpool and the big cities educated folks into a better way of life.'

'No, I think poverty makes folk do terrible things . . . like robbing bodies because they know fine well that a rich man is usually the one that has been more successful than most at robbing his fellow men.'

'Sad! sad!'

'Of course it's sad,' snapped Jackson, '. . . but life is often what you make it, if the opportunity arises most of us would help ourselves to whatever we could, so it's no use being so sanctimonious . . . trust a woman . . .'

'Talking about coffins and burials,' interrupted Abe '. . . I remember a seaman telling me about a time when he worked on a boat on the Clyde. It wasn't unusual for rich seamen, captains and the like, to ask to be buried at sea. Once, a well-known, and rich citizen of Glasgow arranged for his body to be buried in the Firth of Clyde . . . I believe he had spent many a happy holiday on the steamers which took trippers from the city out to Dunoon and the resorts in the Clyde estuary.'

The farmers settled expectantly as Abe began his tale.

'The ceremony was scheduled to take place a long way out in the Firth and the respectable citizen was to be laid to rest on the sea bed. A chaplain of some sort and one or two of the family were taken out by launch and the ceremony was solemnly carried out according to his wishes. Wreaths were tossed onto the surface of the water and the boat turned and made its way slowly and reverently back towards Glasgow.'

'That's a very nice story, it's good to hear that people can have an unusual funeral if they wish . . . anyone can be buried in a cemetery . . . it's more romantic in a way to be buried at sea.'

'Yes,' nodded Abe with a cynical laugh, '. . . it was an unusual funeral all right! . . . as the boat made its way back inshore on the turning tide . . . the mourners were surprised to see the coffin of their dear departed overtaking them on the swift in-coming tide!'

The bar of the Grey Mare burst into delighted laughter.

'My God, that served them right for spending hard-earned money on a fancy burial!' chuckled Jackson.

'How on earth did that happen?' asked an astonished Jean, '. . . surely the coffin should have sunk to the bottom?'

'Certainly it should have done,' replied Abe, '. . . but the men who had prepared the coffin must have thought that the lead needed to sink it would provide a tidy bit of pocket money for them! And it wasn't a bunch of hard-bitten sailors who did the robbing this time. It was a firm of highly respected funeral directors!'

The warm laughter lapped across the cosy bar followed by a comfortable silence.

A silence broken by Alan Steel challenging the company.

'Any more stories about funerals and coffins?'

He glanced in Jackson's direction.

'I thought you might have some sort of coffin tale to tell us Jackson.'

The old farmer slowly finished his pint, then leant back in his chair as an air of anticipation filled the bar.

'You know it's funny how death can be entertaining

. . . unless it's your own!' Jackson observed as he began his tale.

'I was talking to a friend of mine as we walked back from the graveyard today and he was telling me about a relative of his who lives near Wilton, whose uncle had died a year or two back, in America.'

Tom nodded sympathetically, '. . . aye, a lot of families emigrated to America in the hard times, my uncle did the very same thing . . . he's still there, but it must be awful to die, like the Portuguese, across the Atlantic far away from the place where you were born.'

'That's just what Bob's uncle felt, so he made plans for his own death.'

'This sounds interesting,' said Abe, as his pint was refilled, '. . . there wouldn't be much he could do about it, I mean death has a way of finalising most things that we plan.'

Jackson nodded in agreement. 'Yes, he realised that, but like I was saying . . . Bob hadn't heard a thing from his uncle in twenty years. But one morning just as he had finished milking the couple of cows he has . . . you know that they keep only a couple of house cows up there on the slopes of Dent Fell, sheep being their main stock . . .'

'Aye, that's right,' agreed Tom, 'but go on with your tale.'

'Well, to his surprise, he spotted a smart chap in a black suit and black hat making his way up the track to the farmhouse. You can imagine how surprised he was.'

'It would surprise anybody,' agreed Tom, his pint untouched. 'I bet he had brought a letter from his uncle.'

'Don't be so daft,' snapped John Steel '. . . postmen don't wear black hats!'

'The gentleman asked could he speak to the farmer and his wife in the farmhouse privately. Bob was intrigued, such visitors are rare in the countryside. However, once they were settled at the kitchen table the man explained that he was a lawyer acting on behalf of Bob's deceased uncle Mr William Singleton who had died in America only a few weeks earlier. Uncle Bill had made a lot of money in The States and wanted his ashes to be returned to the farm where he had been born . . . and scattered on the fellside. The solicitor explained that should this be possible he would return the next day with a parson and the urn of ashes which was at the moment locked up in his office. They would then scatter them, with all due dignity across the fellside in the way that the client had directed. Of course Bob was only too pleased to welcome his relative's remains.'

'Had he left him any money? That's the most important bequest he could make!' observed Alan drily.

'Aye, after a bit of reflection, that's exactly what Bob thought. But the solicitor said that his client had made no such gift to his nephew.'

'Mean old bugger!' exclaimed Abe Mossop hotly, '. . . I would have told that fancy solicitor where he could put his ashes!'

'Aye, well, like I was saying, the gent in the top hat returned in a couple of days, along with a parson, and carried the urn, with great ceremony, across the farmyard, through the gate and up onto the fellside. They seemed to be chanting prayers or something as they walked along.'

'I should think so too, I'm glad somebody thought about laying the poor man's remains to rest in a Christian way,' said Jean icily from her position behind the bar.

Jackson continued his account unaware of her comment.

'What neither the city gent nor the parson realised was that slowly walking across a farmyard carefully balancing a container in your hand is very enticing to the hens and ducks who are used to that sort of ceremony at feeding time.'

Laughter rippled around the bar in anticipation of what the outcome was to be.

'Of course neither of them turned round, they were too busy muttering and mumbling, and were unaware of the parade of hungry poultry following close on their heels. At last, when they reached an outcrop of rock they stepped up onto what was a natural pulpit, and looking out across the valley, they ceremoniously released the contents of the urn, allowing the particles to float gently on the wind hopefully to reach their last resting place.'

Jackson paused as his audience waited, anticipating the climax of the tale.

'But Bob's hungry hens had other thoughts . . . I doubt if a single speck of Uncle Bill rested in peace in his place of birth.'

'I think that's one of the saddest stories I have ever heard,' retorted Jean, but her charitable thoughts were drowned in the waves of laughter.

'No tale tells as well as a true one,' laughed Alan, '. . . I think Peter Garret can truly sleep in peace, seeing as how we've all laid him to rest in a spot safe from grave robbers and such like.'

'Aye,' said Jackson airily, '. . . his body and soul are safe enough, because, fortunately like most of us, he left this world as he came into it . . . with empty pockets!'

11

A QUESTION OF JUSTICE

The bar of the Grey Mare resounded to the laughter and the animated rise and fall of the customers' voices.

Jackson and three of his friends were playing dominoes on one side of the room, their glasses of ale within a comfortable arm's reach. The clientèle, mainly farmers, kept a lively conversation moving around the bar – discussing the livestock prices at last Thursday's Auction Mart in Whitehaven.

Sudden bursts of laughter punctuated the flow of comments, as first one, then another, recounted how he had outwitted some unwary cattle dealer . . . or had bought a bargain.

'I only bought the cow out of pity,' boasted Harry Jepson, '. . . them farmers over beyond Bassenthwaite never have enough grass to feed their beasts throughout the winter. All the poor thing wanted was a good feed, and by God, she milked out a treat this morning . . . I reckon that was a good buy . . . eh, Jackson?'

He directed the question to the old farmer who was contemplating his hand of dominoes quizzically. Slowly he looked across at his questioner.

'It's time you had a bit of luck Harry, because I know that, as a rule, you're a poor judge of a milking cow. You're like a lot more of these younger farmers around here . . .'

His glance coolly washed over a group of younger men who were lined up at the bar, '. . . a big bag is all you think to look for . . . and that's not always the best sign. Take them Ayrshires you're all keen to buy these days . . . when they stop milking you're left with a heap of

112

bag, belly, horns and bones!' Jackson glanced up again. He knew perfectly well what had been sold the previous Thursday.

'Yes, but how did you know I bought a decent milker Jackson?'

The old farmer lowered his dominoes below the edge of the table before he replied.

'It was when you said beyond Bassenthwaite Harry. Good milking Ayrshires wouldn't survive in that rough country, they need the easy grazing they have in southern Scotland . . . it had to be a decent cow . . . them poor farmers can't afford to keep anything unproductive . . . an expensive cow can ruin the family.'

'I didn't know that you knew so much about farming as far north as that Jackson!' exclaimed Joe Watson in a semi-reverent tone as he cradled his dominoes in his hand.

'There's a lot you don't know about me,' replied Jackson, '. . . anything I do know I didn't learn from the pages of the "Farmers' Weekly".'

'I've seen copies of the "Farmers' Weekly" in your house often enough,' triumphed Harry.

'Aye, but who did you see reading it? It wouldn't be me. Our Bill buys it . . . he's like a few more . . . he's always looking for ways of farming that don't get his feet dirty.'

The old man warmed to his subject and his audience warmed to their entertainer. They knew that a provocative remark aimed in his direction was guaranteed to liven the evening up.

Jackson's regular visits to the Grey Mare was prized events, that is, if he was on form.

Jackson responded to the encouragement. '. . . they're all gentleman farmers, our Bill thinks if he reads all those articles it'll tell him how to be a successful farmer. What he doesn't know is that all these chaps had money *before* they started to farm . . . for many of them it's just a hobby . . . proper farmers like me and Tom Graham never appear in farming magazines . . . we're too busy farming!'

'You're too bloody ugly to be photographed for a magazine,' quipped Harry, as the customers enjoyed the joke . . . but a confident Jackson continued unabashed '. . . think of all the time it takes to get dressed up . . . then keep clean long enough to have a photo taken! You mark my words . . . somebody else must be doing all the real work behind their backs.'

'Talking about Tom Graham, where is he tonight?' asked Alan Steel.

'He had to take Mary to see her mother, who's in bad fettle.'

'Owt serious Jackson?'

'I don't think so Alan . . . but you know what mothers-in-laws are like . . . they have to have a bit of attention every now and again.'

At this point he turned sharply towards Joe Watson who was seated on the other side of the domino table.

'Well, how long is it going to take you to lay your domino Joe? You seem to be miles away . . . you're not sickening for anything are you?'

Joe, who had been gazing absent-mindedly at his hand, jerked himself back to awareness and placed his domino on the table.

Bill Brown and Alan Steel both placed their pieces on the table. The game was over. Alan, the winner, turned to Jackson. 'Not so lucky tonight Jackson, what was wrong?'

'A bad hand Alan, it's the double four . . . always an unlucky domino . . . I knew I'd lost the minute I picked it up . . . no chance with that in your hand.'

'Never mind,' soothed Alan, 'I see the police were at your house yesterday . . . what have you been up to?'

'You don't miss a bloody thing . . . he only called for a bit of advice . . .'

'Advice! On what?' exclaimed Harry who was now listening with renewed interest.

'. . . on a subject you know nowt about . . . conservation of wild flowers . . . and suchlike.'

His listeners laughed at the very notion, but Jackson continued undeterred.

'Aye, that young policeman from Egremont police station came to tell me it's time I dressed my dykes, but he went back to the station informed that my overgrown hedges were doing a fine job for the conservation people.'

'You crafty old bugger! I would have liked to have been one of the flies on your ceiling, listening to that crack.'

Jackson, however, wasn't listening to Alan, he was looking keenly in Joe Watson's direction.

'How about another pint Joe? You've been moping about like a sick calf all night . . . what on earth's the matter with you?'

'Well,' confided Joe, '. . . I have a problem . . .'

'A shopkeeper with a problem!' laughed Jackson, '. . . you don't know what problems are. Neither rain, drought nor blight concern folks like you . . . the queues of construction workers from the camp keep you busy . . . atomic energy keeps you comfortably in business Joe . . . I don't know where they get the word *energy* from . . . they all have cushy jobs. Come on Joe, if your problem is how to spend the money . . . then we'll help you to make out a shopping list of your own.'

Bill and Alan both nodded and muttered in agreement.

'No, Jackson, my problem isn't making money . . . it's keeping it long enough to put it in the bank . . . I was robbed again last night . . . all my takings gone as well as cigarettes and chocolates . . . what a mess the place was in this morning.'

'What about the police?' asked Bill.

'They say because I live opposite my shop, and not on the premises it's very difficult for me to hear intruders. All I can do is to lock and bolt the doors securely. The trouble is that the police station is so far away that it takes a long time for them to get here . . . and by that time the thieves have disappeared. All I'm doing now is ordering stuff for them chaps to come and pinch whenever they like . . . eight times I've been robbed this year already.'

'Aye, aye,' sympathised Alan, '. . . at least we don't have your problems Joe, . . . I wish we could help . . . but I reckon your only help is the police.'

'Police! police!' stormed Jackson, '. . . police! that's where you made your mistake! You must remember Joe, that the policeman is the servant of the law . . . no more . . . no less!'

'But we need the law Jackson,' argued Bill, '. . . the law protects us . . .'

Jackson laughed derisively at this naive statement, '. . . you, Bill, are like the eighty per cent of the population of this country who mistakenly believe that the law has been written for the benefit of the community as a whole . . . oh, no Bill . . . you just tell me who . . . writes the law . . . studies the law. . . and who lives by it . . . just you answer me that . . . any of you?' he added his glance embracing the row of listening faces.

'The police?' volunteered Abe Mossop who was leaning against the bar.

'Oh, no, not bloody likely! *He's* the servant of the law, as I said before. A policeman cannot interpret the law . . . only a criminal can do that! No, Abe, the policeman only does as he's told. *He* knows what to do *after* the crime's been committed but he can't help you with *crime* prevention.'

Jackson turned his attention to Joe Watson, '. . . that's true, isn't it Joe? No wonder you're worried . . . you need some sound advice.'

'How about a solicitor?' asked Alan, '. . . there's a good one who got my brother John off his dangerous driving charge. Very efficient he was, I thought John was all set for a term in prison after that old lady stepped out in front of him . . . she's still in hospital.'

'Now, that's what I've been trying to tell you. Who lives by the law? That's the answer . . . Alan's just provided it. It's them solicitors that live by the law. Don't make the mistake of confusing *justice* with the *law* my friends . . . there's no connection.'

He settled himself with his new glass of ale, then continued '. . . John Steel is the living proof of that . . . we all know he's a menace in that car.'

He addressed his remarks to Alan, '. . . the worst thing your John ever did was to sell his horse and trap and buy a car. The horse had a bloody sight more road sense than him.'

Even Alan joined in the laughter as an unperturbed Jackson continued his appraisal of the law.

'No, a solicitor survives *because* of the law . . . whereas the policeman gets his pay whatever happens. Every solicitor has to make sure that his client can pay him . . , guilt or innocence is matterless . . . in fact . . . a guilty client is often far more useful to him than an innocent one.'

'Come on Jackson, you're talking rubbish!' laughed Abe as he passed the replenished glasses of ale around.

'Rubbish! Oh no, Abe, that solicitor from the city rubbed his hands when John Steel walked in . . . they're clever, very clever. It wouldn't take *him* long to discover that John has more money than sense! He's an ideal client . . . one that's likely to be back a few times . . . and, my friends . . . chaps like John can afford to pay well for their mistakes!'

A murmur ran round the bar as the drinkers considered this cheerful slur on John's character. But as Alan was smiling the sense of anticipation returned to the assembly.

'And another thing to remember that's in favour of the solicitor,' continued Jackson, '. . . is that, in this country the accused is innocent until proved guilty . . . that gives him a head start on the prosecution.'

When the laughter had subsided poor Joe spoke up. 'Where does that leave me then Jackson? Everybody certainly has a head start on me.'

'That leaves you in the position where the only person who can help you . . . is yourself! . . . if you have no idea how, then you might as well pack it in now, sell the stock you have, and look for a job at Sellafield . . . but if it was me . . . I wouldn't let my livelihood be stolen like that.'

'What would *you* do then Jackson?' asked Joe who now had a more hopeful look on his face.

'Just you listen to me Joe . . . once . . . a few years back now . . . when I had some fine laying hens. I was plagued to death by a fox . . . a cunning old bugger . . . not only did he steal to eat, but he slaughtered as many as he could . . . for pleasure. There was no regular pattern to it . . . but it was happening far too often for my liking. So, I decided to get rid of him. Three nights I sat up waiting for him . . . and, my God it was cold! On the fourth night I saw him sneaking across the field. I pulled the trigger! He never took another step! I protected *my* livelihood all right!'

'Good God! Jackson! I can't *kill* anybody to save my shop! It's not the same as killing a fox!' pleaded poor Joe.

'That's right,' agreed Alan, '. . . no one gets hanged for killing a fox in this country . . . haven't you got a better idea than that?'

Jackson raised his hand to lull the laughter, then continued his explanation, unabashed by their hilarity.

'Who said anything about *killing*? I fully intended to kill the fox . . . because there isn't a hospital in this country yet that fixes up injured foxes . . . with a fox it has to be a life or death decision! But, with a man, it's a totally different question.'

He glanced briefly along the listeners lined the length of the bar, '. . . I hope you chaps notice that us farmers are thinkers as well as doers . . . most folk can only do one thing properly . . . but some of us have to be more versatile than that!'

He turned to a puzzled Joe.

'It all depends on how good a shot you are. A man is a bloody sight bigger than a fox's head . . . to *kill* a man you have to have made a bloody *big* mistake! That's why we've won most of our wars . . . we were worse marksmen than the Germans . . . panic shooting can be deadly all round!'

'But when it's dark . . . it's hard to take aim,' said Bill.

'No problem there, as far as I can see,' snarled Jackson impatiently, '. . . you said that the chap had climbed through the window Joe?'

Joe nodded.

'Well, I'm sure of one thing . . .'

'What's that?' asked the confused shopkeeper.

'He can only climb through . . . head first . . . is that right?'

'Yes, I suppose so.'

'So . . . you wait until he's in the process of climbing in . . . then, when you're sure that his arse is pointing your way . . . you let fly . . . it'll take him a good while to die from a shot at that end of him! Time enough for an ambulance to get from Whitehaven hospital! So, there's little risk of the chap dying!'

'He'll only be charged with manslaughter I should think,' volunteered Alan reflectively.

'Your John only got a fine,' retorted Jackson, '. . . and he nearly killed an old woman who wouldn't think of stealing a penny from a soul. All you need is John's solicitor . . . pay him well to be proved innocent . . .

remember what we said ... all criminals are innocent until *proved* guilty in this country.'

Jackson shuffled himself, ready to make his way to the door.

'Well, that's your problem solved Joe, and it's also the end of my last pint ... if I don't get myself away home our Edith'll have locked the back door ... come on Patch, we're off.'

At this Jackson stood up, reached for his walking stick as his excited dog popped from under his chair and stood waiting with eager eyes for his master to open the pub door.

* * *

A couple of weeks later the farm had been busy for an hour or so and the family had now made their way to the breakfast table.

'What a lot of traffic went by our gate last night, did anyone hear it?'

'Not me,' Jackson answered his wife, '. . . I go to bed to sleep . . . I leave the night-time activity to them that can sleep during the day.'

'I thought I heard a police car, or an ambulance flying by twice,' said Jane anxiously.

'It'll be Anne Steel, her baby is due any day now,' observed Edith hopefully.

The barking of the dogs heralded the arrival of a visitor, a look of surprise crossed the faces at the breakfast table – it was a little early for social callers. However, the sound of Tom Graham's clogs soon announced his familiar step.

'Come straight in,' invited Edith. She could see his dog Spot already racing Patch and Flash round the farmyard in noisy welcome.

'You're early this morning Tom, sit down and Edith'll pour you a mug of tea and find a bite to eat for you.'

'Here you are,' said Edith pouring the tea while Esther lifted a couple of slices of bacon and a thick piece of fried bread onto an empty plate for their visitor.

'Taste that Tom, I'm pleased to see you've come across to try a bit of our bacon this morning, there's no rubbish found its way into that pig's trough,' said Jackson as unconcerned as though a visit before breakfast was a daily event.

'Thanks Jackson, I finished the milking as soon as I could this morning, I'd run out of cigarettes.'

'Aye, it's well seen that you never worked down the coal pits Tom – you would have learned to chew tobacco like me – it would have saved you going all the way to the shop – I always have a good stock in.'

A pity he left the pits Tom, the money was better and regular . . . not like farming when you never know what money you will have to spend from one week to the next . . . but it's nice of you to call on your way home.'

'I called to give you the latest news.'

'What's that?' Edith felt instantly anxious.

'A shooting . . . at Joe Watson's shop . . .'

'A shooting! is anyone dead?' asked Esther in amazement.

'No,' Tom replied as he demolished the last of his bacon, '. . . not dead, only injured. Joe was waiting up with a shotgun. I expect he got tired of the break-ins . . . he'd been watching for a good few nights . . . from his bedroom window . . . watching and waiting for the thief!'

'Is the man badly hurt?' asked Jane.

'Not really, he'll live . . . shot in the hip! He must have been in the process of climbing in.'

Edith had to sit down during the conversation, the shock was too much for her.

'I'm surprised at Joe Watson,' she gasped, '. . . I never thought such a thing would have entered his head . . . what on earth possessed him to do such a terrible thing?'

'God only knows . . .' agreed Tom, '. . . but everyone reaches a point when they've had enough, and Joe must have reached it this last week.'

'What's happened to him?' asked Edith uneasily.

'Taken him to the police station I suppose . . . they can't leave a chap with a gun on the loose!'

'I never thought he had the guts,' observed an unusually silent Jackson.

* * *

Jackson was busy raking up the last traces of hay in a field which bordered the main road. Just as he and Peggy reached the hedge he glanced up the roadway and caught sight of a bicycle and uniformed rider approaching him in the distance. It was Bill, the police sergeant, Peggy had already decided it was time to stop for a chat.

'Glad to see you cleaning things up a bit Jackson,' remarked the policeman as he glanced across the field.

'You know me Bill, I always have next year's growth in mind . . . this lea will grow through nicely by summer.'

Bill laughed. 'Yes Jackson, I'm well acquainted with your *conservation* policy!'

Jackson's eyes twinkled as he remembered Bill's young protégé who had called to advise him that his dykes were getting a bit overgrown.

'We still have the pleasure of his company,' laughed Bill anticipating Jackson's question, '. . . incidently, talking about police matters . . . I was in court this morning . . .'

Jackson paused uneasily as he tied the last rope over his bouncy load.

'You were?' he queried, well aware that Joe Watson's case was to be heard that same morning.

'It was a fair hearing,' Bill paused, observing the farmer's heightened interest. He nodded, then repeated

122

'. . . a very fair hearing . . . and a very fair verdict . . . I think the police detective handled the incident very tactfully . . .'

'The verdict Bill! . . . the verdict! . . . what did he get?'

'Two years.'

'Two years! My God! . . . two years in prison for defending his own property? Where's the justice in that?'

Bill smiled indulgently at the incensed face glaring at him.

'Two years *probation* Jackson!'

Calm returned to the farmer's face with a speed which defied challenge.

'Let me see . . .' continued the bemused officer, '. . . ah, yes, . . . two years probation . . . and a promise to be on good behaviour . . . the latter was guaranteed by his solicitor.' Bill swung his leg over his bike as he finished his account.

'He's a lucky man Jackson to have found such a good lawyer!'

'Yes,' agreed Jackson as he reached for Peggy's bridle, 'yes Bill, it's a wise man that gives advice . . . but it's a wiser one who can take it!' he called to the departing back of the pedalling policeman.

12

WELLIES

'**M**y Goodness!' Exclaimed Aunt May as she gingerly picked her way through the farm scullery.

'What on earth is wrong?' Asked Edith anxiously, fearing that her sister had spotted something which might be considered distasteful.

'I never thought I would see the day when you would buy yourself a pair of Wellington boots Edith! I can see that they're yours by the size . . . and I must say that as you apparently *have* to wear unladylike footwear on a farm . . . these are a definite improvement on the rough, dirty, noisy clogs you have worn for so many years.'

The smile was still on her face as she took her usual chair near the roaring fire in the farm kitchen.

Jackson looked up from his morning paper and smiled back, pleased that his fault-finding sister-in-law was in such a good mood.

The reason couldn't possibly lie here on the farm. She must be bringing happy news from Egremont, perhaps the Queen was about to visit the district again. Only news of that kind would bring such a benevolent atmosphere into the kitchen along with May.

'Nice to see you on such a fine morning. I can see you've come all this way to cheer us up . . . push your chair closer to the fire, Edith'll have a pot of tea ready in a minute or so, and you can give us all your news.'

May's beaming face turned to a perplexed one as she absorbed her brother-in-law's cheerful welcome. Somehow lines were being crossed already. May was instantly suspicious of any favourable welcome from the cantankerous Jackson.

'No, Jackson, it's a strange thing if I can't visit my own sister without being questioned as to whether I'm delivering all the tittle-tattle from the town! Goodness me! You'd think that I stood about the street corners collecting gossip to turn over at the first possible opportunity!'

Edith placed the teapot near to her sister's cup and swiftly proffered a plate of tasty sandwiches in an effort to calm any brewing storm. Slowly the dancing earrings settled as their mistress poured a grateful cup of tea and warmed her chilled legs at the fire.

'I'm sure Jackson would never ask you to repeat any gossip May. He knows as well as I do that you would never lower yourself to either listen to, or repeat anything that was unseemly.'

She turned to Jackson who had now raised his newspaper to a height where he could glower and fume in comfort.

'May noticed my new pair of wellies as she came in Jackson and said how much she approved of my changing to modern footwear after all these years of working in clogs.'

She turned back to her sister having failed to raise the slightest glimmer of response from her indignant husband.

'It was Esther who persuaded me to buy them. One of my own had split down the middle and was nipping my foot. She explained that all farmers' wives and daughters are replacing clogs with wellington boots now . . .'

'I'm glad someone in the family has the right idea!' snapped May, lowering her cup and glaring in the direction of the unrecalcitrant *Daily Herald*.

'*If* women *have* to work on the farm among smelly animals and muddy fields, then at least they should do their best to keep as smart and fashionable as possible. There's no excuse for letting yourself go just because you are forced to help to run your husband's business.'

Both earrings stirred into a frenzy of annoyance as she spoke.

Edith felt alarmed as her husband slowly lowered his paper to confront the sparking eyes of his sister-in-law.

'Them bloody stupid boots have caused more trouble on this farm since our Edith was persuaded to buy them a fortnight ago, than enough. If I had anything to do with them, I'd toss them onto the back of the fire . . . nowt but a danger to the stock and everybody working around them.'

'How on earth can you say that Jackson?' asked May unperturbed by the farmer's rising temper.

'It's just like *you* to imagine drawbacks simply because somebody is trying their best to update things on this nineteenth century farm.'

'I don't care what century we're in May,' snapped an enraged Jackson, slapping his open hand down sharply onto the trembling table.

'Our cows don't bloody well know what century it is . . . all they know is . . . that until them boots sneaked into their byre they knew where everybody was. But now they have no idea when Edith might be creeping about.'

'All they have to do is look behind . . .' announced May triumphantly. 'Cows can turn their heads, even when they're tied up . . . and they all have good hearing . . . at least those that are under twenty years old! Any over that can't kick anyway . . . as you well know.'

Jackson's temper knew no bounds. He was grateful that his children were safely out working on the farm this morning, he wouldn't like them to have witnessed such a slanderous assessment of animals they considered to be almost family pets.

A rich slice of cream cake provided the respite which Edith had silently prayed for.

'Jackson will get used to them in time, May . . .'

'It's not a question of *me* getting used to them Edith,'

retorted her husband angrily, '. . . it's a question of *"the stock"* getting used to them. All our animals have been used to hearing us clatter around them in noisy clogs . . . that way, they don't feel that we're springing any surprises on them. They know by the sound whether we're bringing feed or coming to milk them or to let them out. Let me tell you . . . that Maud has been the nearest to a nervous breakdown that I've seen her. She's always been difficult to settle down . . . but now all that silent sneaking about has reduced her milk to half a bucketful less than usual.'

'You know that she isn't far from calving again Jackson,' remarked Edith her pleading tone asking for a truce in her kitchen.

'Just you think what a struggle we'll have with her then!' snarled an incensed Jackson, '. . . she'll be dancing all over her stall for weeks . . . I reckon we'll have to sell her if we're to restore some sort of order in the byre.'

'You do exaggerate things Jackson,' ventured Edith timidly, '. . . things aren't as bad as that, all our stock isn't like Maud, she's an unusual animal.'

'You think so?' asked a surprised Jackson. He turned in May's direction. '. . . she hasn't told you about the first morning when she wore them rubber things . . . has she?'

'No, she hasn't, she's had no chance to say anything so far,' observed May coolly.

Edith's puzzled face could only gaze back helplessly, unable to follow her husband's train of thought under this attack.

'There you are May! Edith can't even remember the state the pigs were in when she went to feed them on that first morning.'

Edith was about to reply to this apparent calumny but was forestalled by her husband's ready explanation.

'The poor hungry buggers had no idea that their breakfast was on its way . . . they were all fast asleep in the warm corner of their hull . . . and it wasn't until they *smelt* the hot pig feed as it slopped into their trough that they had any idea what was going on!'

'You do tell lies when it suits you,' snapped Edith, angered by her husband's version of the events.

'. . . and as for feeding the horses . . . I wouldn't dare ask her to try! Imagine the kick she might get from Captain if he was startled out of a comfortable doze by an unknown creature creeping into his stall. He might think it was a couple of rats sneaking under his belly to steal scraps of feed he had left in his trough.'

'Nonsense!' snorted May. 'All the animals know our Edith well enough and wouldn't dream of harming her.'

'Unlike you May, I would prefer not to take the risk. Just think what you would say if you landed here one day to find Edith with her leg in plaster and all the housework waiting for a kind visitor to do it for her! I'm only thinking of the family as a whole . . . somebody has to take the responsibility for the actions of a lot of shoe designers who put profit before safety on busy farms.'

He nodded self-righteously and reached for his stick and cap.

'I must go and let them calves out . . . they've been waiting to hear my clogs cross the yard for the last hour or so. I won't have any trouble waking them up, they'll be waiting to pop out through that hull door like a bunch of startled rabbits.'

'Take no notice of him, May. He likes to hear himself talk. Come and see the new dress Esther bought at the week-end. She's been invited to a wedding next month and I'm sure she'd like you to see it.'

* * *

Peggy came to a stop before her master could speak. A next door neighbour travelling in the opposite direction was exactly what she'd been hoping for, just a pity the cart was empty and the reins were held firmly so that she couldn't sneak a bite of tasty grass from the side of the road. But a little nuzzle with Lady, Tom's friendly mare, was still a welcome alternative. Peggy wondered if humans were aware of their horses' need to meet friends of their own. She doubted it . . . they were always too busy being friendly with their own species to notice what their horses might need.

'You're a late starter this morning Jackson!'

'Aye, well the wife's sister came so I couldn't just walk

out and leave her. I felt that I had to spend an hour or so making her up to date with what's going on down here.'

'Aye, there are times when a chap has to be sociable just to keep things moving on smoothly in the family Jackson. When Mary's mother comes she likes me to be there to put in the occasional word or so. But she's a lively old soul and is always ready to learn something more about farm life ... I can't say we've ever had wrong word since the wedding day.'

'Well, I can't say the same for May, but she responds to explanations ... so long as I keep it all simple and straightforward. You have to make allowances for townsfolk who don't know any different. I call it education Tom ... at times it seems uphill ... but usually I can make her see the sense in what I do. Today she was asking about them new rubber wellington boots I bought Edith when her clogs packed in after no more than five years wear ...'

'Oh yes, she would take some persuading that times move on and in spite of the expense you would have to find the money ... I've had the same problem at our house. Mary was very unwilling to change. She reckoned that clogs were drier and warmer than thin wellies, but in the end she saw that I was right ... she's never had wet socks or bits of hay and straw stuck under her feet since she started wearing them.'

'Aye, Tom, you're right! It takes a thoughtful, concerned husband to notice these things and keep our wives dressed in the latest and smartest working gear. Come on Peggy, let's go and snag some turnips ... we'll have to sell something if we're to keep the womenfolks dressed in the height of fashion!'

'He's always in a hurry,' snorted the mare softly to herself ... 'can't he understand that we need to have our conversation as well?'

'*You* can stop *your* snarling as well,' said Jackson addressing the mare, '... the women of this world seem to gang up on a chap ... who only seeks to please the lot of them.'

Peggy rattled her bridle in disapproval.

13

Duty Free

'**A** good pint of ale tonight Jean.'

'It's a good pint every night Tom. I think maybe you've had a long busy day today and the drink tastes better.'

'That's right Jean, circumstances can alter things a lot.'

'How can such an idea be true Jackson? Good beer is good beer whatever a chap's been up to earlier in the day!' laughed Alan Steel.

Jackson lowered his glass ready to meet this challenge offered by his long-term adversary.

'Now Alan,' he began, settling himself more comfortably in his usual chair by the fire, '. . . it's a funny thing when we consider our enjoyment. Just you look back on the times when our womenfolk have been most pleased! I bet it was when they've managed to buy a bargain!'

'What's that got to do with enjoying a good pint?'

'Just you wait and listen for a few more minutes and I'll explain. As you know, if your Anne bought an expensive frock . . . then spotted another woman wearing the exact same thing . . . and she discovered that she had paid a few pounds less than Anne had for it . . . do you reckon that she would enjoy wearing it after that?'

'No, women are funny that way. But I still don't see what all this has to do with enjoying a pint of ale.'

Jackson continued his explanation, unperturbed by the interruption.

'The opposite is true if she buys something which turns out to be cheaper than the same one bought by a neighbour in Whitehaven a month before! By God Alan! She won't half enjoy wearing that particular frock! She'll say it's the best dress she's ever bought. When it's worn she'll even sew it into her next patchwork quilt . . . she'll put it in a spot where every time a chap's about to fall asleep he's forced to admire this particular bit of dress.'

'I'm still waiting to hear what all this has to do with a good pint of ale.'

'Aye, we're all wondering what the connection is,' agreed Tom uneasily.

'The point I'm making is a psychological one, that is . . . that enjoyment is all in the mind.' He paused to poke the fire into a bit more life, illuminating the listening faces as he did so. The customers in the Grey Mare knew that some unlikely reminiscences were pre-occupying the old farmer's thoughts.

'Enjoyment . . . enjoyment depends on several circumstances being in place. Take, for example, the shipwreck off the coast of St Bees . . . if must be years ago now.'

'A common thing in those days Jackson,' snapped Alan, 'most of the beams in our houses and barns are from ships that foundered off these shores. They say that the Irish Sea is bad to negotiate in a gale . . . but anybody that's daft enough to go off to sea has to risk being either sunk or shipwrecked . . . but I still can't see how all this tale is going to explain Tom's decent glass of ale.'

'Just you have a bit of patience and listen a little longer Alan,' continued Jackson, 'and enjoy that expensive ale you've got in front of you.'

Alan nodded, pleased that he'd goaded the storyteller into justifying his remarks.

'It must have been in the early part of this century, if I remember rightly, when some barrels of Porter were washed up on Coulderton beach.'

'Aye, I've heard my father talk about that,' laughed Tom.

'Well, as you all know, the Customs & Excise Office in

Whitehaven had to be informed and they always came and took such a cargo to be impounded in the Custom House down there on the dock.'

'Yes, that's the law,' nodded Tom, '. . . but I bet it would take a long time for such news to reach Whitehaven.'

'On market day, we all could be there for an eight o'clock start, but it's funny how no one could find time to make it to Whitehaven to inform the authorities!'

'It could be at least a couple of days before the officers got wind of the stuff that had washed ashore!' chuckled Jackson.

'It bet it tasted good! . . . isn't Porter a type of beer. I've never tasted it.'

'Yes it is Tom . . . but you have answered Alan's question very well, it wouldn't matter if you were tee-total, you would still find a free sampling undeniably tasty.'

'I've paid for my ale,' said Tom, still puzzled.

'Aye, so you have . . . but if you'd never tasted Porter in your life, you'd still have thought the barrel you'd picked up on the beach was the best drink in the world. But, you know, at that time there was a woman called Sally who enjoyed a pint or two . . . of anything!'

'Unusual for a woman to drink in those days Jackson.'

'True enough Abe, but Sally was a regular shopper at the back door of a good few pubs in Egremont. She'd carry a jug underneath her shawl and the landlords were always pleased to fill it for her.'

'What a pity women can't enjoy the warmth and crack in a pub like you men do. It's another example of the unfairness of life for a woman.'

'Come on Jean, a chap can't afford to keep everybody in the house in drink. Women have enough luxuries coming their way as it is.'

'That's right,' agreed Abe Mossop, '. . . we've got to have somewhere we can have a serious talk . . . without a stream of complaints and criticisms coming our way.'

He turned in Jean's direction, '. . . and just you think of the nonsense you'd have to listen to . . . a collection of women gossiping about the price of eggs . . . and how long their permanent wave lasted!'

'Can't have been very permanent then!' laughed Jackson. 'But you're right . . . talk like that would give women like our Edith notions they never had before. No, I reckon the everlasting life they promise in the "Mothers' Union" is the right outlook to encourage in our wives.'

The men laughed, appreciating the safety of these remarks.

'You were talking about old Sally . . .' Tom reminded his friend.

'Oh, aye, so I was . . . well, the Customs & Excise officers never received the slightest hint of the ship-wrecked liquor for at least two days. But the barrels had been spotted one Sunday afternoon, kinda' late on . . . and Sally was seen making her way down to the shore, her shawl wrapped warmly round her head and shoulders . . . God knows what she had hidden beneath all those folds! We know she had at least one big pint mug.'

'What a long way to walk for a drink! It is at least four miles each way. She must have been a dedicated drinker!'

'She was that Alan! But the old lady had no intention of walking a round eight miles or so each day . . . that would be wasting good drinking time.'

'Did some kind person in the village take her in?' asked an intrigued Jean as she dried the glasses behind the bar.

'What a daft question!' snapped Jackson, 'no . . . she spent all of the three days, until the Customs men came, drinking as much as she could.'

'What did she do at night? What did she eat? And, there are no public toilets down there on the beach . . .

and there'd be plenty of men about swallowing as much of the free stuff as they could.'

'Trust a woman to think of complications! Who wants to eat if there's plenty of drink to enjoy? As for night time . . . we all need a rest if we're to enjoy the daytime drinking . . . and there's plenty of snug hollows beneath the railway embankment. Old Sally would be safe enough down there. As for a closet . . . all she had to do was to cross the railway line and she'd have all the privacy she wanted. Men loading the barrels wouldn't dream of going out of their way to cross the railway line . . . by the time the "Customs & Excise" chaps found their way down to the shore only a few token barrels were waiting for them . . . with not a soul in sight. They had probably passed old Sally happily plodding her way back to Egremont. They would never guess that the poor old country woman had swallowed more of the king's ale than the king himself could swallow in twelve months!'

'Serves them right . . . the duty on drink is ridiculous. You'd think the few pleasures we working men have would be reasonably priced.'

'Aye, you're right Abe . . . it's a good story . . . just a pity that the most dedicated drinker there, was a woman!'

'The best of reasons Alan for discouraging our women from coming into pubs,' nodded Jackson, '. . . we men realise that women aren't built to be serious drinkers . . . we know that things can go wrong . . . just like they did for old Sally. A kind guiding hand in her vulnerable years would have saved her from a lifetime of degradation and possibly a lonely death in the workhouse down in Whitehaven.'

The men nodded pleased to hear such words of wisdom.

'A kind guiding hand early on might have saved you all a few pounds,' snapped Jean, but her comments were

ignored by the self-righteous group of drinking soul savers.

*   *   *

The wind whipped Captain's tail sharply against his hocks as Jackson stopped the two horses on the lofty cliff top.

'Why can't he stop us close to the gate where it's not so chilly and the grazing's a bit tastier. There's no understanding humans!' thought the gelding to himself.

He glanced sideways at Peggy – but she seemed to be content with this uncomfortable perch. Maybe there was no understanding older horses either!

Captain rubbed his nose craftily on the front of his fetlock . . . maybe these green things growing near his feet were tasty.

A sudden tug on his bit returned his wandering nose to its rightful place.

A reproachful glance from a half-dozing Peggy settled him to a hungry wait.

Jackson wrapped the ploughing cords firmly round the handles of the heavy plough used for splitting the stitches where the young potatoes and turnips grew.

A rest was welcome and he liked to pause on this bank top and enjoy the vista across the encroaching Irish Sea. This vantage point allowed a clear view all the way from the southern marker of Black Combe, north to the Scottish coast, across to the Isle of Man as well as inland to the towering Wasdale and Ennerdale mountain ranges. What a landscape to contemplate!

It always amazed Jackson that a port like Whitehaven with its strong tradition of seafaring should be so close to areas of farmland where people had little interest in life on the sea. Most like him, had to wrest a living from the land, or beneath it, travel to distant lands was unknown to them.

Still, this panorama unfolded beneath him was always fascinating. Distant settlements over in Scotland were usually clear, as were the outlines of the hills on the Isle of Man.

Jackson settled himself on the cliff top to eat his sandwiches and enjoy his bottle of cold tea.

He glanced at the hind-quarters of the two horses. He knew it would be easier to enjoy the view if those two couldn't graze their way from him as they liked to do.

The year was just warming up and the surface of the sea seemed to be smiling with a chuckling ripple moving across its upturned face. The dark shadows marking the seaweed-covered rock pools lying beneath the water, hid from the naked eye, the battles waged for food by the shrimps and crabs who populate these dubs.

Jackson wondered if the view from this vantage point, right to the bottom of the water was anything like that seen by a pilot as he flies low along the coastline.

Strange how travel has been so important to man. The tale in the pub last night, the story about the shipwreck and the barrels of ale floating ashore.

What if he, Jackson, possessed a holy rod like Moses in the Old Testament and could order the Irish Sea to dry up for a day or so! What interesting wrecks would he find scattered on the sea bed, their treasures unveiled for the first time, resting alongside the dead bones of the sailors keeping eternal guard.

He shivered, making Captain push back both ears to monitor his master's intentions.

Reading in the 'Geographical Magazine' he understood that there were hills and valleys complete with forests of underwater kelp and weed where fishes swim through the swaying tops like birds do in the sky, a wonderland hidden by a blanket of moving water.

Ships had made their way across these waters over the centuries, protected by the closeness of the land. Only the marauding Vikings had sailed along the coasts to plunder the rich land. It must have been a terrifying thing for the coastal villagers when they spotted the approaching fleet of Norsemen intent on murder and rape.

'We border families must have been bloody tough,' he observed out loud.

Captain took one step forward anticipating his master's command.

'Stand still, can't a chap make a remark without a daft horse deciding to run the show!'

Captain relaxed, his nose nuzzling against Peggy's for comfort. She shook her head sharply . . . young horses have to learn to know their place in the order of things.

This fertile coastline must have always looked inviting from people passing at sea, thought Jackson. At school he had heard how a young girl missionary, St Bega, had landed here and built the abbey at St Bees. Even a holy woman could see that this was an ideal place to settle. Religion always went down well, especially with the womenfolk around here.

Take the Irish who had settled here during the last century. They fled from the potato famine in Co. Antrim and Co. Down and they had found plenty of work in the mines here. They must have heard that Cumberland was one of the best places to settle. I suppose we got the more intelligent ones, thought Jackson, the daft ones went all the way to America . . . silly buggers . . . they can't have known that there was a decent living to be had almost within sight of their own shores. After all, we had traded with them for years, cattle from Ireland in return for coal from the pits near here. Aye, the sensible ones ended up here.

Most visitors to our shores were decent, law-abiding traders, who brought rum and tobacco to Whitehaven . . . not like the bloody Scots. He'd read how Robert the Bruce had sneaked in the back way and had slaughtered almost the entire population of Egremont at one go. Aye, he thought sadly, at least you stand some sort of chance if you spot raiders coming in from the sea, but a band of wild scotsmen sneaking round the side of a mountain after dark, bent on killing honest working townsfolk, doesn't give anybody much time to do bloody much about it.

Jackson rose stiffly to his feet as a southbound train pulled into the tiny station. 'Carlisle to London in no time at all' he mused as he turned back to his ploughing, '. . . the old border raiders wouldn't half have enjoyed stepping on a train in Scotland then flying through the border lands, and a few hours later stepping out in

London . . . a spot where they could have practised their pillaging among the really wealthy citizens of England!'

Peggy and Captain were both instantly awake, ready to pull in the direction of the gate, and more hopefully, home.

'Thank God I've only got you strong-willed buggers to deal with!' laughed Jackson as they all moved off in unison. The powerful plough sliced into the flattened ground lifting the soil into a neat, even, furrow to create a deep bed where the young plants would grow strongly through the spring and early summer.

The startled train whistled as it left the station.

'A right muddle of ancient and modern passengers wouldn't half liven the long journey to London!' laughed Jackson his imagination running riot! Imagine the modern passenger with his concerns about connections and tickets sitting opposite a raiding Scot bent on a quick pillage then a ride back to more fighting at home! Born to fight! he laughed to himself, then as he recalled the rapes in ancient Egremont, he reflected that maybe there was a lot more scots blood flowing through his veins than he thought! Maybe a bit of mixing up makes for a better cocktail, he thought as he heard the distant whistle as the train neared Braystones station.

14

HALLOWE'EN

'You're late tonight Alan. We reckoned that roan heifer had started to calve.'

'No, Anne persuaded me to make a bloody fool of myself trying to eat an apple hanging by a bit of binder twine. God knows who first thought up these daft games, just because it's the night witches are supposed to ride about on broomsticks . . . or something daft like that.'

'Hallowe'en, that's what it is tonight,' volunteered Jean from behind the bar, '. . . it's the night that ghosts and witches come out to frighten folks.'

'It doesn't have to be any special night when the wife's sister decides to cast her beady eye on what an innocent farmer happens to be thrang with . . . she doesn't even need to be fitted with a broomstick . . . the bus fetches her any day of the week . . . except Sunday,' snapped Jackson, '. . . anybody who believes that only the dead appear to trouble us must have a better set of in-laws than I have.'

'I shouldn't be so quick to dismiss the idea that unnatural events can't happen,' said Abe Mossop '. . . there's some spots I wouldn't like to be in at midnight on a black, dirty night like this.'

By now the pub was filling up with a few miners who had come from the town to pass a couple of hours or so enjoying the crack in the 'Grey Mare'.

The firelight glinted on the faces, some sporting a permanent reddish hue from the ingrained metal ore they worked with. A voice growled from a corner seat.

'It's brave talk sitting here in warmth and comfort . . .

but I can remember going fishing down the Ehen not far below the old church at Beckermet.'

'What happened Dick? Don't tell us you met a ghost?' laughed Tom Graham, a little uneasily.

'Stan and me had decided to do a bit of night fishing . . . and we were walking back . . . a bit later than we'd planned . . . and as we walked along the path near a bit of high dyke, the old churchyard came into view. My God! but it wasn't half dark and gloomy, everything seemed to be swaying, it was hard to tell which was shadow and what were branches, walls or headstones. The whole lot appeared to be changing position, like a sort of macabre dance. We thought the tower leaned towards us as if to warn us off its territory.'

'You'd never catch me in a spooky spot like that on a dark night,' announced Bill Brown, as he felt a slight shiver running down his spine.

'Don't be so bloody daft . . . nowt that's dead can harm a chap . . . it's the living we have to fear.'

'It's alright talking like that Jackson, but I reckon that strange things have been known to happen . . . go on Dick, finish your story.'

'Aye, well, whatever anybody says, it was bloody eerie down that lonning. By that time we were ready to believe owt! Neither of us spoke, but each one knew that the other felt exactly the same . . . we'd be damned pleased when we'd passed the church and reached the car that we'd parked in the edge of the main road. Then . . . just as we were walking by the churchyard wall . . .' he paused to relish the expectant looks on the drinkers' faces, not a single glass was raised, each hushed, waiting for the end of the tale. Only the noisy crackling logs ignored the progress of his story, prepared to snub any creditable outcome.

'. . . suddenly we heard a loud flapping and, glancing over the wall we saw a white shroud billowing and advancing towards us!'

'My God! What was it?' asked Jean, waiting, unwilling to reach out for the dirty glasses which had been placed on the far end of the bar.

'We didn't wait around to find out . . . fishing rods, tackle and heavy waders made no difference to our speed . . . without a word to each other we raced down the path, threw our waders into the back of the car and drove home as though all the devils in Hell were on our heels!'

'That's a stupid tale,' laughed Jackson '. . . are you telling us that some poor dead soul had managed to lift the lid off his coffin . . . burrow his way up through six feet of heavy soil, then have the strength to jump over a church wall and chase a couple of daft fishermen, bloody stupid, if you ask me . . .'

Dick drank his ale and then smile wryly as the company settled to their forgotten drinks. Then he continued his tale.

'In a way you're quite right Jackson, we found out when we went back the next day to look for a good fishing knife Stan had dropped by the wall, that the gravedigger had been opening a grave and had left a large white sheet over a bush near the wall to dry!'

'And you daft buggers thought a ghost had made up its mind to frighten you?' chuckled Alan Steel warming his hands at the glowing hearth.

The drinkers in the 'Grey Mare' laughed in appreciation of such a plausible and reassuring story.

'That story reminds me of what happened to me when I was a good bit younger and lived in Whitehaven, up behind the workhouse and the old cemetery.'

'Tell us about it Arthur,' invited Abe Mossop eagerly, but at the same time glancing uneasily through the window into the gathering darkness.'

'It was soon after I started working at Sellafield. I hadn't been long left school and it was an early start often on dark mornings. It meant leaving the house at half past six then walking down the hill to the station to catch the Sellafield train. Usually us young uns met one another on the way down and reached the station in a group just in time to reach the platform as the train came out of the tunnel into the station.'

'It can be very dark on winter mornings and plenty of company is welcome,' agreed Ben.

'That's right ... well, as you all know ... the workhouse is right next to the cemetery and the road runs below a high retaining wall, the graveyard being higher up than the roadway. But as I was telling you, one dark morning as we lads were hurrying past ... late as usual ... we heard a voice calling *"help me down ... help me down ... give me a hand lads ..."* We looked up, and there perched on top of the high wall the figure of an old man dressed in a long white nightshirt holding a skinny arm out towards us ... we thought he'd climbed out of his grave!'

The pub burst into spontaneous laughter. Arthur waited for the chuckles to subside then continued ...

'I have read about a chap that's run a mile in just under four minutes ...'

'That's right he's called Roger Bannister, I think.' volunteered Tom.

'... well I can tell him that us daft lads made the mile to the station in less than four minutes years before he did! We did it without the benefit of special shoes ... a level track ... or a following wind!'

'What did you run like that for?' asked a thoughtful Jean, '... who could possibly be afraid of a poor old man who must have wandered out of the workhouse into the cemetery, then wanted a kind passerby to give him a helping hand to go back to his bed?'

'Come on Jean,' snapped Jackson, 'they were a bunch of lads ... and lads are noted for acting first, then stopping to think,' he paused then continued his observations '... especially folks from Whitehaven. Have you

never heard of miners who turn back home if they meet
the Newtown boggle on their way to the pit of an early
morning? ''Bad luck!'' they say . . . but it's an excuse to
have a shift at home . . . particularly on a Friday
morning. Friday was a popular day for the boggle to take
an early morning walk!'

'At least these lads ran *to* work instead of back home,'
laughed Abe.

'Aye, they say every generation should be an improvement on the last,' explained Jackson, 'and it seems to be
working out that way in Whitehaven.'

Arthur accepted the free pint offered him with a smile
then continued his narrative . . .

'It was the only time we reached the station before the
train had even left Workington! How's that for a record?'

'Weren't you scared to pass the cemetery wall after
that?' asked Jean as she pulled more drinks.

'My mother laughed when I told her the story . . . and
I felt stupid as I realised that it wasn't a ghost but just an
old chap in a nightshirt wanting a hand down . . . you
know I've never told anyone about it before, but as a
chap gets older he can laugh at himself, but I must admit
that all of us were always pleased when we'd passed the
graveyard!'

'What sort of jobs could a bunch of useless lads do at
Sellafield?' asked Abe sceptically.

'Tea boys we were,' said Arthur proudly, '. . . you
remember it wasn't an atom place then, it made
explosives, it was a TNT factory. We were paid 30/– for a
five and a half day week. It worked out to be a twelve
hour day with the long travelling time added – but we
finished at dinnertime on Saturdays . . . then went to a
football match in the afternoon. That was the treat of the
week for us in them days, we enjoyed the work even
though it was such a long day.'

'A long day! A long day!' snarled Jackson indignantly,
'. . . you should have thanked your lucky stars that you

hadn't to go back to do the milking on a Saturday night and twice on Sunday, like we have to!'

'Say what you like about it Jackson, but I'm glad that things have got better over the years. We couldn't have a doze in the middle of the afternoon if things were a bit quiet, like you farmers can.'

He paused, realising that he was treading on sacred ground. Thankfully Ben interrupted to tell another tale.

'I reckon that true stories are always the best. A few years back Tom a friend I work with had to go on a business trip with another chap from the factory. They had to spend the night in a hotel in Prestwick in Scotland. So, after they'd got settled in and had a bite of dinner, they made their way to the bar to have a crack with the locals, he said there was a pleasant friendly atmosphere, so he struck up a conversation with one or two folks around the bar. The other chap with him called David, spotted an old man, a sea captain who was sitting in a huge high-backed armchair over in a far corner of the bar by a curtained window. As he had always had an interest in the sea he walked over and asked if he could join him. The old chap was delighted to have somebody to listen to his tales. He was a retired captain and told David stories of when he had captained ships during the war on the Russian convoys. David heard how the decks and superstructure of his ship had been so weighed down with the layers of ice formed by the water crashing over the ship that the crew had to work like demons to chip it off in case it tipped, then sank the ship. He recounted how he had landed at the Russian port with a cargo of machinery that was so heavy that it couldn't be lifted from the quayside . . . and was still there long after the war . . .'

'What a waste! Men risked their lives for such pointless reasons,' sighed Jean sympathetically.

'. . . aye, that seemed to be the truth of things, David had sat listening to the old chap's reminiscences until well after midnight . . . enjoying every minute of it. Mind you there were plenty of funny stories about life at sea to be told as well as the tragic ones. But the crack had put in a few entertaining hours for David, and when at last he rose to go up to his room the bar was deserted, Tom must have got fed up with waiting for him.'

'I would like to have heard more about the Russian convoys,' mused Abe, '. . . but is that the ghost story you are telling us?'

'No, I haven't finished yet. It was like this . . . the next morning when David and Tom met at the breakfast table, Tom was furious, "You were an unsociable bugger last night. These bloody Scotsmen thought I'd brought a religious hermit across the border with me."

'David was astonished, "I spent the evening, as you well saw, talking to the old sea captain sitting in the big armchair by the window. He cracked on about his wartime experiences . . . he told me how he'd captained ships in the Russian convoys during the war!"

' "Don't talk so daft! I saw no ship's captain . . . all I saw was you sitting next to that big empty chair all night . . . sulking and not saying a word to anybody! The next time I have to travel away on factory business, I'll make sure that I go with somebody who . . .'

"Excuse me, Sir" interrupted the waiter, ". . . but I couldn't help overhearing what this gentleman was saying about chatting to an old ship's captain. Can you describe him?"

'David described his companion as meticulously as he could. He related the story about the convoys and said how he'd been fascinated by the tales the old man told.

'The waiter was very agitated as he listened to David's account.

"Have you perhaps stayed at this hotel before?"

"No, this is the first time I've ever set foot in Preswick."

'David felt uneasy as the waiter's face turned a shade paler than it had been.

"Why?"

"Because, old Captain McDermot passed away last October and he used to sit in that chair and relate his experiences with the Russian convoys to anyone who cared to listen! Few people care to sit in that chair, it seems a cheek to take his seat!"

Ben glanced round the listening drinkers, incredulity patterned on their faces.

'Now that's a believable ghost story,' said Abe Mossop quietly, '. . . there's more things happen on this earth than we can account for. They say there's ghosts that wander about in Muncaster Castle . . . we don't have to go as far as Scotland to hear such tales.'

'Aye, ghosts don't have to frighten the life out of unsuspecting folks . . . otherwise the Pennington family would have taken themselves off to live in one of their other big estates, I believe they have one in Scotland.'

'Yes Alan,' agreed Jackson, '. . . but maybe the Scottish ghost is more frightening than the ones at Ravenglass. I should think that dead Scots can be every bit as cussed as the living ones! Anyway, ghosts living in a great rambling castle shouldn't be a scrap of bother to anybody. It's only in little houses that things can get a bit crowded . . . then I suppose an awkward-minded spectre drifting about could become a bloody nuisance!'

Jackson stood up and made for the bar to renew his pint still nodding his head in disbelief at Ben's story.

'You chaps believe any rubbish you're told . . . now I have a friendly horse that's kept in that field not far from the bus stop . . . and, would you believe it? . . . one dark night when Edith's brother came to spend a few days with us . . . to concrete that heifer byre . . . he landed at our house in a right state. He reckoned that he was just walking along after being dropped off by the last bus, when he spotted a strange shadowy shape moving about behind the dyke near a gateway. It was making a moaning sound and swaying about. Silly bugger! He'd run a good half mile before he realised that there was nothing chasing him! I guessed that Captain would still be having a good laugh to himself after he peeped over the top rail of the gate!'

Jackson returned to his seat still chuckling.

'Are you never scared about anything supernatural Jackson!' asked a laughing Alan Steel.

'Good God, no! . . . maybe I should be though because the prospect of becoming a roaming ghost certainly appeals to me . . . it beats singing hymns and flapping a pair of white wings for eternity.'

'Well!' laughed Tom, '. . . the best thing for me about Hallowe'en is the number of turnips I sell on the market. I always sell a cart load, even them that's gone bit rotten inside sell well . . . at a lower price, of course, because they're easier to hollow out. Mothers buy them to make Jack-o-lanterns for their kiddies. No, I've no quarrel with witches and hobgoblins, the more the merrier if you ask me!'

'I think you chaps have sat here long enough discussing the para-normal . . . it's time to close the bar . . . gentlemen.'

'Have you room for one more passenger in your car Ben?' asked Arthur hopefully, '. . . it's a bit far to walk home at this time of night.'

Jackson laughed gleefully, '. . . are you scared of meeting a few witches, dead sea captains or even a playful horse on the way home Arthur?'

'None of them bother me Jackson, but I've to be up in good time in the morning to catch the early train to Sellafield!'

15

ESCAPE

Jackson looked down below his feet which were placed firmly on the shaft of the cart, and idly watched Peggy's hind legs as they swung along, her feet seeming to bite into the tarmacked surface of the road.

He settled himself as comfortably as he could though he was perched on the front of the cart, his back supported by the bags of freshly milled corn which formed his load this morning.

Jackson allowed the reins to lie relaxed across the horse's swaying spine knowing that he could allow his mind to safely drift from the task in hand. His outward journey early this morning, to the mill in Egremont had been a battle of wills between him and the mare every inch of the way! The slightest pull against her shoulders had instantly produced a lowering of her head, laboured snorting gasps of weariness accompanied by trailing leaden feet! To any other road-users, unaware of the deviousness of a workhorse's mind, she painted a picture of an over-worked, miserable animal in need of a prolonged rest in a lush pasture.

This return journey had, however, produced a miraculous rebirth of energy! The crisp rocking of the speeding cart began to have a soporific effect on Jackson who had risen very early in the morning to get the milking finished in order to be in good time to load up for the mill. Not so his mare! His eye followed the line of lively muscles along her back and flanks working rhythmically beneath the leather gear ending with the ears pricked eagerly forward as if to escape from the sharp ringing sound of her hooves.

Jackson always enjoyed these trips to the mill, even though it meant a half day's work. The crack had been good, he had learnt what the quality of this year's crop was like throughout the district. This load of feed would keep the stock going for a good bit, then as usual, the battle of wills would have to be fought once again. Maybe an unsuspecting Captain would be a better bet next time! But he knew that Peggy was completely unflappable in the busy streets of the town when she had to tethered near to the noisy rattling corn mill. He wouldn't dare leave such a young untried horse as Captain in the care of a lad while he enjoyed a pint in the 'Black Bull'. No, cussed as she could be, Peggy was his safest companion.

As he basked in the pleasure of this interlude of peaceful rhythmic rocking, he had just begun to speculate on the tasks at home awaiting his return, when the lumbering sound of a double-decker bus approached from behind. Peggy shook her bridle in annoyance as Jackson pulled her over to the left to allow the bus to overtake them more easily.

'For goodness sake behave yourself,' he snapped in the direction of the unheeding ears, '. . . you'd think you owned the road!'

The bus slowly overtook the horse and cart and a number of the passengers waved a cheery greeting in Jackson's direction. As he returned the greeting he could feel Peggy increase her speed as if she resented any vehicle reaching her farm before she got there.

'I might just as well have caught the bus in Egremont,' he mused '. . . this bloody mare could have brought herself home!' Suddenly his eye caught sight of a large hat with tiny roses along the brim . . . that hat looked familiar . . . good God! he was sure it belonged to May, Edith's sister. No other person from the Egremont area could own a hat the same as Aunt May's . . . that was an impossibility! Jackson hadn't been able to catch a glimpse of the face beneath the hat, it had been turned studiously away from the horse and cart. 'Then it must have been May' he said aloud to himself. 'And you needn't break your neck getting us home soon either,' he observed to the deaf mare, '. . . there's not a thing to hurry home for . . . especially if that snobby old bat's waiting to tell me how to improve Edith's lot.'

A welcome silence wrapped itself around the swaying cart as he watched the bus, privileged to carry his sister-in-law, disappear over the next hill.

Jackson's not so happy thoughts were soon interrupted by the appearance of a shabby ancient pick-up chugging and panting its way up the long hill towards him. When it eventually drew alongside Abe Mossop leaned out to have a friendly word with Jackson who was having the devil of a job to rein-in the reluctant Peggy. With ears pressed hard back and her rump held firmly against the breeching strap to hold the load against the slope, Jackson attempted to talk to his neighbour.

'I've got those two saddleback gilts in the back, the ones I was telling you about. I decided to sell them to that chap from Haile who's been after them for ages.'

'Aye, a good idea, I don't know why you've waited so long. That boar you have is their father, so you'd better buy in some decent gilts from somebody else!'

'Well, the truth is that it's the missus that's the problem! She's grown awful fond of them two pigs. She reckons that I should sell the boar and keep the gilts . . . But I've told her that we run a farm, not a bloody pet shop! Anyway, I'll be off, I can see that your mare'll pull your arms out of your shoulders if you have to hold her on this hill much longer.'

Jackson gradually released his grip as he steadied the mare and load to the bottom of the slope. He didn't even have time to return Abe's parting salute as they both struggled off in their respective directions.

'He doesn't have to fight with that engine like I have to fight this bloody home-sick horse . . . you're like them two saddlebacks . . . ruined by the women in the house. Maybe an obedient tractor wouldn't be such a bad idea after all.'

Peggy ignored her possible redundancy happily pricking her ears forward and stepping out like a young filly.

I don't remember Edith saying that May was coming today. She usually likes me to be at home to treat her like an honoured guest . . . being sociable she calls it. Perhaps it hadn't been May on the bus . . . but she had a hat like the one he had seen. He chuckled to himself. He would delight in telling her that someone on the St Bees bus had an identical hat. He remembered it well, because she'd hung it on the back of the kitchen door and the cat had taken a fancy to its swinging ribbon, luckily Edith had spotted the wicked glint in the cat's eye before she pounced.

Come to think of it, they hadn't had a visit from May since before she went to Blackpool with the 'Mothers' Union' or some such group. He believed she said she might meet a nice gentleman at the tea dance in the Tower ballroom. Perhaps she'd struck lucky and was coming to make wedding arrangements! Unlucky, though, for some poor chap who probably looked forward to a peaceful life at the end of his days, not a continuous round of wiping his feet, being sure which drawer to put his socks in and remembering which of the neighbours to ignore! Perhaps he should warn any possible suitors.

Suddenly a movement in the dyke-back a good distance ahead caught his eye, returning his straying thoughts to the task in hand. It looked like a couple of dogs trotting along in the same direction as Jackson, maybe a couple of trail hounds who'd missed their way. Peggy's ears registered curiosity as they switched from long to medium wave as they drew alongside the rummaging figures.

'Dogs bedamned!' said Jackson aloud as the two animals took a clear shape, '. . . them's Abe's two gilts, the doors at the back of his van are always tied up with binder twine . . . I bet them two little buggers managed to bump against them, broke the twine, then jumped out! He would never hear them for the noise of that spluttering, coughing engine, I've heard of "homing pigeons" but never of "homing pigs"!'

The two pigs grunted a careless greeting in the direction of Peggy's flashing feet, but continued their trotting, nuzzling journey in the certain direction of Jane Mossop and their feeding trough.

The happy pigs were soon left behind . . . a delighted Jackson contemplating a pig story on his next visit to the 'Grey Mare'! Then, equally happily, his mind switched to contemplate Abe's arrival in the farmyard at Haile! What wouldn't he have given to be there about now as Abe proudly walked to the rear of his van . . . only to discover that his pigs had flown! They'd managed to escape at some point along the five mile journey. As far as Abe was aware it could be anywhere . . . at this very moment they might be racing up Egremont Main Street . . . or crushed to the thickness of prime bacon under the wheels of the St Bees bus! The opportunities for hilarity were endless! Of one thing he was certain, Jane would never part with her pigs now, Abe'd have to sell his boar, and, what's more, he wouldn't dare try to take that wicked bugger in the back of his old van! It would take one of Bill Bates' expensive trucks to transport it to its new home. Already in his mind's eye Jackson could hear Abe moaning on over the next twelve months, about the transport bill, and telling the entire pub what trouble he was having with his new boar! As if everybody else doesn't have the devil of a fight with any boar they might keep.

Peggy snorted gently as she approached her farmyard gate as though she too was chuckling at Abe's dilemma.

'Slow down, or you'll collect that stoop . . . it would serve you right if I unloaded this crush, then went back to collect them two pigs. But the bother of catching them, then keeping them safe and settled in the cart is too much for both of us, if they can escape once they can escape a second time. Apart from catching the bus they'll be home as fast on their feet as any other way!'

* * *

'Nice to see you May' greeted Jackson, a happy smile on his face, '. . . I thought I saw you on the bus.'

'I didn't see you Jackson, I was admiring the countryside . . . early summer is so beautiful . . . buttercups and daisies carpeting the fields in every direction . . .'

'Some seem to have strayed onto your hat, that's how I knew it was you. I didn't think I had seen anybody else wearing a hat like that.'

'I should think not! I bought it in a proper milliner's

shop in London, I wouldn't expect to see such a fashionable hat in this area!'

'Take no notice of Jackson, May, he doesn't know anything about ladies' hats, he never notices when I wear a new hat.'

'New hat? We can't afford such luxuries! Now just look at that cap of mine' he nodded towards his worn milking cap resting innocently on its peg on the back of the kitchen door, '. . . I bought it long before the war, and I expect it to last as long as I'm farming.' •

May wrinkled her nose as her eye considered the treasured headgear of uncertain colour.

'It looks as though you bought it before the Boer War not the last war, what colour was it when you bought it?'

'Who said anything about the last war? I was talking about the Great War. They made things to last in them days, as for the colour . . . I can't rightly remember what shade it started out as, but it must have been one of the shades of cow shit . . . because I've never noticed it change, it's just as useful as the day I bought it . . .'

Eyes and earrings registered the flicker of shock simultaneously.

Edith hastened to avert an explosion of revulsion.

'Never mind your dirty old cap Jackson, eat your dinner while May gives us all her news.'

Jackson ignored the suggestion and continued his appreciation of the milking cap, '. . . it's like this May . . . once a cap gets past its smart wear, if it's any good it usually makes a useful milking cap. Now if I threw it away I'd have to break in another one and that's always a long painful job . . . the cows get used to a chap's head pushing against them wearing the same cap, it's sort of . . . familiar to them . . . a good sharp neb lets them know who's boss in the byre.'

Jackson tucked into his dinner, and, unperturbed by Edith's anxiety continued to address his sister-in-law.

'Now, May did you pass a couple of black and white pigs on the road from Egremont? They were coming this way, I reckon you must have overtaken them somewhere.'

'Pigs? pigs! I'm not in the habit of noticing pigs! And, I'm not sure that pigs go for walks either. I think you've been living among animals too long Jackson, perhaps you should think about buying a nice little house in Egremont . . . it would restore you to a more normal life . . .'

'Has somebody's pigs got loose?' asked Edith embarrassed by her sister's comments.

'No, Jane Mossop's two saddleback gilts decided that they didn't fancy living up at Haile . . . so they jumped out of his pick-up and were making their way back home when I overtook them. Abe'll get a surprise when he pulls into the yard and tells Jim Dixon that he's fetched the pigs he's bought!' he chuckled at the thought, '. . . just to discover that the two little buggers have jumped ship! I reckon they didn't want to change their life style.'

'The way you talk, you'd think that the dirty creatures could think for themselves.'

'You don't have to be very intelligent to know when you have the best of troughs. Jane Mossop was breaking her heart this morning when Abe drove her pigs out of the yard, and I'm sure the gilts think the world of her as well. No, May, animal psychology is as deep a study as any human psychology. The next time you tuck into a plate of eggs and bacon, remember that you're enjoying a piece of thinking, feeling animal . . . "Best Bacon" . . . isn't just a meaningless slogan you know!'

'May was about to tell me how she enjoyed her trip to Blackpool.'

'Oh aye, let's hear all about it May. Did you meet any nice folks? Better still . . .' here his eyes twinkled mischievously, '. . . did you meet any suitable gentlemen?'

To his surprise, May blushed slightly under her discreet makeup.

'Tell us about it May . . .' coaxed Edith.

'I was asked to sit next to John in the bus . . . he had joined the group at Cockermouth.'

'I thought it was a "Mothers' Union" trip. I didn't know that men joined.'

'Men are welcome, they come with their wives . . . but . . .' here she paused coyly, '. . . but he's a man of the cloth . . . a widower.'

Jackson's eyes widened as they absorbed the shock.

'Good God May, you can't bring a vicar into the family! We don't have enough china cups or embroidered tablecloths to cope with a man of the cloth . . . have we Edith?'

'Of course we have . . .' gasped a delighted Edith, ignoring her husband's barbed observation, '. . . tell us how it all happened May.'

'He's a charming man, with impeccable manners . . . and an unerring feel for the waltz . . .'

'Doesn't sound like a vicar to me May. Have you checked up on him? I didn't think vicars were expected to feel anything!'

Edith's glare silenced any further enquires.

'. . . he was charming to all the ladies . . . but it was me he asked to dance more often than his other partners . . . I think it was that dress you altered for me Edith, he said such grace of movement was a delight.'

'How nice!' soothed Edith, '. . . has he suggested meeting you again?'

'That's really why I decided to come all this way to see you today.' May reached into her handbag and pulled a letter from its capacious depths.

Jackson's eyes were riveted to the missive.

'I've never met a chap who conducts his courting at a distance!' he observed . . . intrigued.

May waved the letter briefly before her sister's eyes.

'He says he has to make a pastoral visit to Egremont next month and would like to call and take tea with me!'

'Have you told the neighbours? You wouldn't want them to think you were entertaining strange men!' asked a serious-faced Jackson.

'Exactly,' nodded May, '. . . I would prefer a chaperone to be there . . . I wonder if you would join us for tea that afternoon Edith? A gentleman caller would arouse less comment if you were seen to be calling the same afternoon.'

Jackson chuckled, '. . . only one month to practise your teatime etiquette and wash all the cow muck off your hands Edith . . . they do look a bit ingrained!'

'Be quiet Jackson . . . of course I'll come May. I will be delighted to meet . . . John . . . let me know the date and I'll be there first thing in the morning, I'm sure Tom would run me to Egremont if I said it was important.'

Jackson's face fell when he realised that Edith intended to be away from the farm for an entire day.

'Wouldn't it be better if you invited him to come here for a day?' he suggested hopefully, '. . . a walk in the countryside can be very romantic you know.'

'What! with dirty pigs escaping from vans and then cavorting along the roads, a gentleman from the town would be shocked to see such irresponsibility!'

Jackson rose from the table.

'Well, May, it's time I was off to push along the raw life we live here,' he chuckled as he reached for his cap, '. . . I'm looking forward to an hour or so in the pub tonight . . . to see if Abe Mossop will try to resell his gilts, or settle for a new boar, that is if he wants to breed a few litters from them. Come to think of it . . . your John might be interested in such questions, doesn't it say somewhere in the Bible that we should "go forth and multiply" . . . but we'll never know the truth of that unless you bring him along!'

'I can't understand what your Jackson's talking about,' snapped May tartly.

'Just you ignore him and tell me more about John,' urged Edith invitingly.

16

A Secret Meadow

As the lonning became narrower and a bit rougher, Jackson decided to dismount from his bicycle. The two dogs, Patch and Flash raced back to check that their master was still coming in their direction.

The walk was very pleasant, made pleasanter by the knowledge that all the hay had been led and was safely stored in the barns. Yesterday had been the last haymaking day and the final loads of the year had been led from these distant fields many of which were located down even narrower lanes which branched off from this main arterial lonning. Anchor lonning snaked across the countryside linking fields and meadows belonging to a good number of farms then eventually joined this network of land and lanes to the main tarmac road.

The surface over which Jackson now wheeled his bike had been well churned up by both the sharp horses' hooves and the cutting rims of the heavy cart wheels. Clear and deep semi-circles were visible where the horses had had to dig into the soil as they had pulled their load up the slopes. Jackson could see the skid marks where the same horses had slid a little as they had held the same loads back on the descending slopes.

His three working horses weren't the only ones who had pulled loads of hay along this lonning during the last fortnight. At hay and harvest-time it became the lively thoroughfare it must have been over centuries.

Carts with rounded loads of hay had taken on the appearance of heavy rocking snails as they had crested distant rises and descents. The horses and the farmers leading these swaying loads had been hidden from a bird's-eye view by the high hawthorn hedges as they plodded along the floors of tunnel-like lonnings.

Today all was quiet, the work finished. Peace rested on the hawthorn hedges so recently bruised and battered by the bulging loads. Wisps of floating hay still hung from their extended fingers, silent reminders of the recent noisy battles with time and weather. Horse-drawn mowing machines, hay-rakes, shouting men and rabbiting dogs had all arrived . . . and in turn, had disappeared allowing these undisturbed fields to catch their breath before the huge binders trundled between the dykes to reach the bigger fields still nurturing the standing corn. Then the pattern of cutting, stooking and leading the loads home, would re-establish itself before abandoning the shorn fields to the welcome tranquillity of, first autumn, then winter. Only a few hardy bullocks and sheep would remain to graze the winter grass.

Jackson turned off the main thoroughfare into a narrow, short branch lonning, muttering to himself as he spotted huge armfuls of his precious meadow hay hanging from the overgrown hawthorns.

'They've overloaded the bloody carts, as they usually do,' he observed aloud to himself, '. . . I tell them every year that this lonning is too narrow for a wide load . . . but they think I won't notice, they're too eager to get the bloody job finished.'

He leant his cycle against the dyke when he reached the end of the lonning and walked into his empty field. The gate had been lifted off its hinges by Bill on the first day before the hay had been cut. That was the usual practice, a hanging or swinging gate (should the farmer be lucky enough to possess one!) would be nothing but a nuisance when wide machinery and loads are manoeuvred between the gate stoops.

He also knew that Bill would have had difficulty if he tried to re-hang it after the last load had passed through yesterday afternoon. He wouldn't have dared to leave his horse and loaded cart standing while he returned to replace the gate. Captain would have set off by himself on the homeward journey, giving Bill the devil of a job to overtake his horse and cart in the narrow lonning before it reached the junction with the main road! Few horses can negotiate a tight turning unaided, so Captain would probably have broken a shaft, a leg, or his own stupid neck as well as giving Bill and the rest of them the hard task of cleaning up the disastrous load.

After he'd re-hung the gate he'd have a quick walk around the meadow to check whether any bits of machinery or hayforks had been left lying about by the careless young workers.

Jackson enjoyed strolling round the perimeter of this rather far-flung meadow. Land that couldn't be seen from the farmhouse was always a bit of a worry, but this little meadow gave no trouble from one year end to the next. Its dykes were high and had been well maintained, so the stock he put in it after the hay had been led would need little overseeing, a weekly visit was usually enough. But he would check that there were no breaks in the dykes.

The two dogs raced ahead, excited to be in a field free of both cows and sheep . . . and with the probability of careless rabbits hopping about.

Jackson stopped. Surely that wasn't the sound of men's voices he had heard? it wasn't possible! Not a mile or so from the main road! He must have been mistaken . . . age brings its own problems . . . its own imaginings! But as his mind settled itself to its own thoughts once more, he noticed that the two dogs were showing a keen interest in the far dyke where he thought he had heard the voices. He'd just walk over there and have a look. He followed the line of the dykes . . . he needn't advertise his presence by cutting across the middle of the meadow.

Sure enough, the voices were becoming louder. Somebody was certainly on the other side of the high hedgerow. What on earth could they be up to? The hawthorn was very thick at that point but Jackson, peering through, could make out two figures engrossed in the foilage. The deep voices told him that they were both men. But their language sounded foreign . . . or was it?

'What a gorgeous origanum vulgare!'

'And here's some fine examples of tripleurospermun!'

Jackson edged closer. He could just see two bespeckled chaps in shorts and carrying rucksacks and what looked like butterfly nets. He caught the odd foreign words . . . myosoton aquaticum . . . succisa pratensis . . . he hoped they would understand his basic English.

'Good morning gentlemen!' he called clearly in his best English.

The startled men looked up into the farmer's enquiring face.

'Ah! Good morning!' they replied in even better English. The elder of the two men spoke up first, 'You must be the farmer who owns these fields . . . we weren't sure where to enquire for permission to explore your hedgerows . . . so we just came along hoping it would be all right.'

'Your English is very good, I could hear you speaking a foreign lanuage as I came near.'

Both the men laughed.

'We're not foreign,' explained the older man, '. . . the words you heard are Latin, names of the rare flowers we are searching for. We are botanists from the University of Durham. We had been told what fine hedgerows you have in this area.'

'So we decided to come and spend a few days studying the flora and fauna here,' added the younger man, '. . . we hope we're not trespassing?'

'No, certainly not,' Jackson smiled broadly at the two men, '. . . I'm only too pleased that you chose my dykes . . . probably the best in the district. I never toss any of that artificial manure in my dyke-backs like them young farmers do with their powerful machinery.'

He paused to introduce himself.

'I'm Jackson Strong . . . and you couldn't have picked a better man to show you our wild life.'

'I'm David Wilkinson, and this is Percy Armstrong . . . we're both professors of Biology.'

'Pleased to meet you.' As they shook hands Jackson envisaged the mileage he could get from this meeting when he retold it all in the Grey Mare.

'This type of meadow and its hedge are fast disappearing . . . that's not surprising considering the pressure put on farmers to plough all their permanent pastures during the war. It takes a very long time for land to be restored to its original quality . . . and usually the wild meadow plants never return.'

Jackson pointed to the far side of the meadow.

'I should have ploughed this meadow during the war, but that area of swampy land over there made it impossible to plough, so this meadow has been preserved. Even Churchill and his men couldn't make us plough through wetlands with water that stands thigh height in some spots!'

The men's eyes widened in delight.

'Wetlands!' they chorused in unison.

'This is much better than we hoped for David!' Percy turned back to Jackson, '. . . may we climb over this hedge and take a look?'

Jackson soon found a gap where the two botanists could climb through, then escorted them to the most unproductive corner of his entire farm.

'Call at the farm if you fancy a cup of tea and a bite to eat,' he called as he made his way to the gateway and his waiting bicycle.

* * *

'Is it true that you invited a couple of professors to come and examine your fields?' asked Abe Mossop a few days later in the bar of the Grey Mare.

'Aye,' added Alan Steel, '. . . there's all sorts of rumours going around this district about you . . . or more likely . . . your Edith . . . inviting them to do research on your land. Why your land? What have you got that's so special?'

Jackson had waited patiently all week for his neighbours' curiosity to surface.

'Well now, lads,' he began cradling his pint against his chest, '. . . you chaps have never read widely . . . nor have you been much good at looking ahead . . .'

'Come on! Stop patting yourself on the back and tell us the plain truth . . . for once!' urged an exasperated, but interested Alan Steel.

'You chaps . . .' he began again patiently, '. . . always wondered why I didn't make a few extra pounds during the war by trying to plough that sumpy meadow down Anchor Lonning. But I knew that a quick pound or two in my pocket might only destroy the special nature of that meadow. What might be a sump to some folks . . . is a special habitat for rare flowers with Latin names . . . to the farmer who has bothered to read about these things!'

'Do you read Latin?' asked Tom in awe.

'I recognise it when I hear it, if that's what you mean . . . all these plants which grow in what you might call . . . neglected corners of our meadows . . . have been well documented in Latin. As you all know . . . Latin is a medieval language spoken by the monks who knew all about curing illnesses by using wild flowers and rare herbs. The well-informed farmer will always be aware of the plant life in his dykes, he knows that no land is pure waste. Because I didn't destroy my flowers with them expensive artificial manures like some farmers did, these two chaps can study my Latin medieval plants . . . and you never know what magic cures they will come up with. The rest of you,' he said accusingly in the direction of the younger farmers, '. . . are only too ready to buy drainage tiles and spend money on so-called improvements to any bits of bog you might spot on your land, which anybody with an experienced eye can see should be left to develop in its own way. One day soon you might read about my meadows in some learned medical journal!' boasted a proud and suddenly eloquent Jackson.

'You'll have to translate the bloody thing for us then!' laughed Abe, '. . . none of us can read Latin!'

'You can laugh as much as you like,' retorted Jackson, '. . . but David and Percy, the two professors, are coming back in a couple of months to look for more rare specimens . . . and I've said that I'll introduce them to a few of my neighbours who might just have a few stretches of neglected medieval-type corners for them to check over.'

Alan's laughter died away as he considered the possibility of his name appearing in a medical journal.

'Yes, Jackson,' he agreed, '. . . it would be a pity to turn these researchers away from the meadows that so many of us have preserved for so many generations . . . they can splash about in mine anytime.'

'And mine.' nodded Abe.

'Well, lads, I wouldn't drive them new tractors about so much . . . they might destroy the valuable flora and fauna which is struggling to grow beneath the wheels,' he warned, his eye sparking with the prospect of dangling such a juicy carrot in front of his impressed neighbours for the next couple of months or so.

17

DISASTERS?

'You look a bit miserable tonight John,' remarked Abe Mossop as he placed his winning hand on the table in the Grey Mare. 'I reckon your mind hasn't been on the dominoes tonight otherwise I couldn't have beaten you so easily.'

'Maybe you could use some good advice, that is, if you have a problem!' laughed Jackson, 'We've always been able to solve tricky personal problems in here,' he nodded in Joe Watson's uneasy direction.

John Steel smiled a bit wanly.

'No disaster pending nor drastic methods needed here! It's just that I feel guilty about that smart pony I've grazed over the summer for our Kate to ride.'

'Why's that? It's a bonny la'al thing,' observed Abe.

'That's part of the trouble, when we answered that advert asking for somebody to keep the pony for the summer with the idea of buying it if we were pleased with it. So we decided we'd like to have her.'

'So, what's gone wrong with the agreement?' asked a puzzled Jackson.

'Well, Kate loves the pony, but a few days ago we received a letter from Manchester, where the owner lives, to say that he wanted the pony back, and he would pay us what he owed for its keep.'

'That seems reasonable,' said Abe, '. . . you knew it was all subject to agreement.'

'Yes, I know that, but last Friday I loaded it into a horsebox and off I went to find the address. I trailed all over that area of Manchester looking for a field or a farm where a pony was likely to be kept.'

'Did you find its home?' asked a curious Joe.

'In the end I had to stop at a phone box and asked the chap to come and direct me,' John paused and sadly reached for his equally sad pint, then continued '. . . soon we reached a busy street with hundreds of houses in a terraced row which stretched as far as the eye could see, not the sort of place to keep a pony, or so I thought. When we stopped I unloaded Crimson and led her down a garden path towards a small house, through a side gate into a back yard . . . and then, believe it or not . . . onto a railway embankment with trains screaming a good twenty feet above! I asked the chap if he'd sell the pony, but he said that a good holiday in the countryside was all he'd wanted for the animal, he'd had no intention of parting with her because she had a living to earn doing small carting jogs throughout the winter.'

'What a shame!' exclaimed an indignant Jean, '. . . fancy the poor beast having to live in a place like that! No wonder you wanted to bring her back with you.'

'Shame be damned!' snorted Jackson, 'You don't understand animal psychology Jean,' he turned to John, '. . . were they about to feed the pony on coal John?'

'No, there was grass on the embankment . . .'

'There you are then, too many of you folks think that a view is important to an animal when it isn't. The beast was probably loved by the whole family. It's not for you or the rest of us to jump to conclusions. That little pony was probably as pleased to be back at home as you were when you drove through your own farm gate late last Friday night.'

'You make me feel better Jackson, maybe I shouldn't have answered the advert in the first place, but I wanted to see if Kate's interest in riding horses would be a lasting one before I bought her a pony of her own.'

'Are you going to buy her one then?' asked an interested Jean.

'I reckon not, she's met a lad at the Young Farmers' Club and seems to be more interested in him at the moment.'

'A bloody good thing that pony escaped back to Manchester and the folks who really care about her then, the only disaster you might have on your hands might turn out to be a son-in-law who fancies not just your daughter but adding a bit of your best land to his!' laughed Jackson.

'That story reminds me of the time when I drove them long-distance cattle trucks for Frank Bates.'

The farmers turned their attention to the speaker, a wiry middle-aged chap who had been sitting listening to John's tale.

'Tell us what happened Jim,' asked Abe, 'I had forgotten that you drove for Frank.'

'That could have been a real disaster! I was taking a load of young stirks to France, they had been brought up on the fellside and, at first, were a bit skittish about being loaded into Frank's truck. But as you all know, they get themselves settled down after an hour or so on the road. When we reached Southampton docks there were plenty of chaps waiting to off-load, water and feed the beasts, and then help me to load them on board the ferry.'

'That must be hard work,' observed Alan nodding sympathetically.

'Usually things work out well, because the animals are ready for a feed and none of them fancy exploring.'

The listeners nodded, fully aware of the docility of most cows in that situation.

'But I hadn't reckoned on that flighty white heifer that had given us all the run-a-round in the farmyard. The minute her nose smelt freedom, she cleared the barrier placed at the side of the ramp from a standing jump . . . and with her tail waving good-bye up in the air, she disappeared in the maze of streets bordering the docks.'

'A bad colour! I've always said white is a bloody bad colour!' observed Jackson chuckling knowledgeably.

'Did you find her?' asked a worried Jean.

'Well, we chased her down one street after another, then eventually cornered her in a school playground.'

'Thank goodness the children weren't out at play,' gasped Jean.

'They were all looking out of the windows. They had heard the police cars with their sirens blaring and no doubt wondered what strange creature had escaped from a zoo . . . you know, they don't see cows down there! But what a lot of fuss was made at the dock when we got her back because Her Majesty's Customs and Excise officers stated that the animal had escaped from the foreign side of the customs barrier!'

'Did they stick an "illegal entry" stamp on her backside then?' asked an amused Jackson, '. . . anybody with an ounce of knowledge about cows would recognise a good English breed! Them French breeds haven't the same "conformation" at all.'

'Good God Jackson, you can't expect a few officers in collars and ties to know the finer points of cattle breeding!' laughed Tom Graham, intrigued by the complications the runaway heifer was throwing up.

'I thought you said something about a disaster,' remarked Jackson, '. . . I reckon you've all had a bit of fun on the dockside.'

'But that wasn't the end of the story. A week or so later, Frank Bates got a letter from a chap who was near the dock on that day. He claimed that the cow had knocked him down just as he was crossing the road . . . on a proper crossing! He was claiming damages for his injured leg stating that he had pressed the button and the lights had shown that it was safe to cross! Someone had read Frank's name on our cattle truck, and he'd tried his luck to get a pound or so compensation out of an ignorant northern trucker!'

'Did Frank pay up?'

'No Alan, he wrote back saying that the chap should sue the Harbour Board for not providing adequate barriers which would be high enough for a dairy shorthorn heifer to clear.'

'I wonder what happened to her ... some unlucky person must have bought a cheeky beast,' mused Tom Graham.

'I read that a white horse came in third at Longchamp last week' chuckled Jackson '... so maybe the French can't tell the difference between a white colt and a white heifer!'

The laughter died down as fresh pints were distributed to the reminiscing drinkers.

'So far we've heard no real disasters,' challenged Alan Steel. 'It's amazing how most happenings have a good side as well as a bad one, but I remember a few years back hearing about a real disaster, it happened on a farm near Cockermouth.'

'Owt can happen over there,' observed Jackson nodding his head wisely, '... tell us your story Alan and let's see if we can make the ending a respectable one for you.'

'As you all know, shearing sheep is necessary, the animals always feel such a lot better when they can gallop about in the hot weather with their thick coat making money for the farmer.'

A growl of disagreement wafted round the bar, with the odd reference to 'when we get the bloody subsidy'.

Unperturbed Alan continued with his tale. 'Well, they tell me that a chap over by Bassenthwaite had his three tups clipped, then turned them out together into the paddock. But he forgot that once the wool has gone the sheep aren't able to recognise each other.'

His listeners murmured uneasily.

'What happened?' asked Joe Watson.

'Well, you shopkeepers won't know that tups that live

amicably together should be tethered apart after shearing until they learn to recognise each other again.'

'So what happened?' asked Jean uneasily.

'Two of them attacked the third and killed him, they banged their heads together a bit rough-like!'

'That was certainly a disaster . . .' gasped Jean.

'Aye, it's more than a disaster it's murder, pure and simple!' laughed Jackson scornfully, '. . . but I would call it "mismanagement" rather than a disaster – serves the chap right, some folks have to learn the hard way.'

'I think that was a disaster,' announced Tom Graham.

'It certainly was for the tup with the thinnest skull,' laughed Jackson.

'You tell us what a real disaster is then,' challenged Alan Steel scornfully.

Jackson smiled to himself then settled more comfortably in his chair, preparing to meet the challenge.

'A disaster is a situation where everybody loses out. Now let me see . . . I'll have to search my memory for a real one.'

'You've shot our stories down Jackson, so you'll have to come up with something pretty serious,' chuckled Alan.

'The only true story that comes to mind is the time that I met my old friend Jack from up beyond Threlkeld . . .'

'Aye, it would have to be about somebody nobody's heard of except a few lonely shepherds who wander about Blencathra.'

'That's right Alan, the likes of us who've never travelled in the Lakes like Jackson did in his youth, won't have a clue whether he's lying or speaking the gospel truth.'

'Trust . . . would be a fine thing for the likes of you Abe,' snapped Jackson, 'a chap tries to give you the benefit of his lifetime's experience . . . and you wonder if he's telling a pack of lies!'

'Get on with it Jackson, and we'll judge how much truth there is in your tale.'

Jackson paused to attack his pint then continued, his tone more than a little injured.

'The story is about a pick-up truck . . . and I haven't seen many shepherds on the top of Blencathra riding about in pick-up trucks.'

He nodded self-righteously in Alan's direction, then continued. 'Jack had bought the truck a good few years back. He had saved hard to buy it, then after eight or nine years or so it started to rust a bit . . . but that didn't matter, it wasn't as though he took the wife shopping in it or anything. Later on, the doors wouldn't shut so he threw them into a heap of nettles . . . it was easier to get in and out quickly without them anyway. The truck had cost him a lot of hard-earned cash so he was determined to get his money's-worth out of it. His wife reckoned it looked a disgrace when he drove it down the main road. But as you will all agree, most wives are pleased to have a pound or so in their hand on market day . . . saved to meet household expenses by a husband who works his machinery until it's a bit shabby instead of throwing good money after bad on something that looks flashy on the main road. Good management I call it.'

'I'm waiting to hear what the disaster was!' laughed Alan, 'we all get our money's-worth out of our machinery, but ten years is a bit greedy if you ask me!'

Jackson turned in astonishment. 'My Clydesdales are only starting their useful life when they reach their tenth birthday . . . and they provide a string of foals to replace themselves! Jack had been used to economic horses, so his coughing and spluttering truck looked like good money being thrown after bad. Anyhow the climax of his misery came one day when he took a load of fat sheep to Cockermouth auction . . .'

'Did the truck breathe its last?' chuckled Abe.

'Not exactly . . . he had put a bit of old gate on the

floor to keep the sheep's feet from paddling in their muck . . . luxury I call it!'

'If he'd cleaned the bottom of the truck out each time he carried stock it would have been more hygienic,' declared Jean.

'Hygiene!' snorted Jackson, '. . . he was far too kind to the sheep as it was. This particular day when he arrived at the auction he opened the back to unload the sheep, but the little buggers wouldn't dream of getting out . . . the grass had grown up through the old bit of gate and they'd grazed all the way from Threlkeld to Cockermouth . . . so one half were having a nap while the other half were trying their best to finish off the good grazing.'

'I'm waiting to hear what the disaster is in that story,' laughed Alan Steel.

'The tragedy is that the truck was on its last legs and it would cost Jack a small fortune to replace it at today's prices . . . as well as having to wait a few years for the grass to grow again on a busy truck floor! Spending big sums of money is the only disaster a farmer has to face. Tin machinery is well and good when it's new, but a chap has to save for a good ten years or so to replace it . . . meanwhile the manufacturers are busy inventing new, more expensive replacements that can put a farmer out of business if the old engine stops before he's saved enough to buy the new shiny monster. The constant worry of finding the money to replace essential machinery is enough to make a conscientious farmer commit suicide.'

'What a good way to keep sheep happy on their way to the slaughter-house,' laughed Jean delighted at the possibility of the tale.

'Aye,' agreed Jackson, '. . . but Frank hadn't the gumption to realise that if he'd thought to plant a bit of mint in with the grass, he could have sold his mutton ready to serve without the customer going to the bother of making mint sauce!'

'The only saucy thing in that tale ... is the teller!'
laughed Alan Steel delightedly.

18

A Wedding

'I don't know what all the fuss has been about. I'm glad that the whole affair is over! . . . I can't even remember who bothered to come when we got married Edith. I just wanted it all over with, then we could get on with our lives. In fact in those days nobody bothered getting dressed up and making such a palaver . . . I think you got married in a pinny Edith, or something that looked a lot like one, didn't you?'

'No, I didn't, but I might as well have done for all the notice you seem to have taken to it!'

'Isn't that an awful thing to say Mam?' said Esther, half laughing, but still not too sure about the truth of the matter . . . she was used to hearing how hard up people had been in the early part of the century. She turned to her Aunt May who had been sitting quietly sipping her tea for the past few minutes.

'What did Mam wear on her wedding day Aunt May? Do you remember?'

'Goodness me, child! You ask such questions! All I remember is that it was a bitterly cold day in November . . . why anyone should choose November to get married is something that I, for one, cannot understand . . .'

'Not much happening at the time,' volunteered Jackson, 'a chap can't waste good weather talking to vicars and relations he hasn't seen for donkeys years . . .' he turned in his wife's direction, '. . . do you remember seeing my Aunt Mary? We weren't sure whether she was dead or alive . . . we hadn't seen her for years . . . and there she was, as large as life . . . her false teeth in . . . all ready for a decent meal!'

'Your family did turn up Jackson,' smiled May serenely,

'. . . it was the only time I had ever met a good many of them. Your Uncle Peter's new boots squeaked when he walked up and down the aisle, they were obviously brand new and probably the only pair of boots he had ever bought. He would have felt more at home if he'd worn his usual clogs . . . and he would have made less noise! By the time he had found the right pew and then got your Aunt Mary Jane settled beneath that awful hat . . . the one that she'd already worn for a couple of weddings and at least three funerals . . . the service was about to begin. But at least they managed to get there before it was all over . . . for once!'

'You wouldn't expect them to arrive on time to every family do, seeing as they live as far away as Nethertown!' said Edith soothingly, glancing uneasily in her husband's direction.

'No distance at all for a chap who has a good a pony as he had, a real mover it was, I seem to remember he called it Cutie . . . and could she travel! No, May, he didn't arrive late simply because he couldn't manage to get there on time . . .'

'In that case what made him late for every family gathering that I ever attended then?'

'It was a question of timing things May. Time is a precious commodity, it's no use squandering it like some folks do. Our wedding was a good example of that very thing. After the ceremony many folks sat in your mother's house for the rest of the day . . . you wouldn't think that cows were waiting to be milked and calves and pigs needed to be fed the way they were busy blethering . . . to say nothing of the drinking that was done by a good many of your family . . . them not being Methodists like most of mine!'

'A pity you hadn't kept that side of the family tradition going!' retorted Edith.

'We were talking about my Uncle Peter, who had the sense to set off for home as late as possible, to save his beasts from suffering from starvation. A great pity other folks hadn't stayed at home and found a sideboard to polish or a grate to blacklead, instead of spying on my relatives . . . that's not religious . . . especially for the good folk who go regularly to the big church in Egremont . . .'

'That's another thing to be thanked for . . .' interrupted a triumphant May.

'What's that?' asked a puzzled Edith, already out of her depth trying to follow the arguments pursued by both husband and sister.

'Thankful that you married in a proper church, not one of those chapel places that are in apology for a good English church, their vicars aren't even vicars at all . . . they never bother to wear clerical collars! Disgraceful!'

She nodded sanctimoniously in her sister's general direction as she continued . . .

'I must say that I had set a good example a couple of years earlier by marrying in the parish church . . . but really there was no problem . . . in George's family there was no trace of any nonconformists . . . both families appear in the Whitehaven and Egremont church registers for generations back . . . pillars of the church we all were!'

'It doesn't matter which church people attend,' soothed Edith, 'just so long as we all live a good life and try to be do the right thing.'

'Aye, making sure the stock is seen to instead of gallivanting off to gawp at folks who have nothing better to do than dress up for a wedding on a cold winter's day, just to please relatives who have decided that the couple should undergo a public ceremony to please, not themselves, but family and neighbours . . . and anyone else who might be shopping in Egremont at the time.'

'Why shouldn't folks pop into the church to see a local couple get married? I think it's very nice to see who's getting married in a small market town like this . . . everybody knows everybody else and it's a matter of interest and goodwill,' said Edith.

'Yes, you're right, I myself never miss either a wedding or a funeral. I always like to show my respect at funerals . . . and weddings are worth popping in to see,' explained May sanctimoniously.

'I bet they are!' chuckled Jackson, 'I'm sure you cast your eye very closely over every bride who dares to enter the church doorway!'

'I'm not sure what you're hinting at Jackson, but if you're suggesting that I would want to add to any girl's shame, then you're very much mistaken . . . a friendly nod and smile is much appreciated. I wouldn't want it to be said that I only support my own family in their hours of rejoicing and sorrow, whichever one it might be.'

'I can't see the difference,' laughed Jackson grimly.

'Come on Dad, weddings are smashing, didn't you enjoy our Bill's yesterday?'

'Of course he did,' smiled Edith happily. 'We were both pleased to see him married to such a lovely girl as Claire . . . weren't we Jackson?'

'I'm not sure whether he was properly married or not.'

'Of course he was,' snapped May, her voice shocked, '. . . whatever made you think that he might not be married properly?'

'Because I never understood a word the priest said! He mumbled all the way through. When I got married I could understand most of the words even if the meaning was beyond the sort of education we got at our school.'

'I've never heard such nonsense in all my life,' exclaimed Edith in outraged tones, '. . . you could have had as good an education as anyone else if you had bothered to go to school regularly, but from what you say you only went when there was nothing better to do.'

'I've always thought there was something lacking in your background Jackson,' said May, a gleam in her eye, '. . . our parents made sure we went to school regularly even though they worked in Africa during some of our childhood . . . you see Jackson the priest was speaking in Latin, that's why you didn't understand.'

'I suppose *you* did? It's the same thing as knowing what sort of tea the Queen drinks!'

'Of course Jackson knew the ceremony was in Latin, we all know that Catholics conduct their important ceremonies in Latin,' interrupted Edith, trying to restore a peaceful atmosphere to her kitchen.

'I think that probably makes sense,' mused Jackson.

'Yes,' agreed May, 'to me Latin sounds dignified and devout, it lends a feeling of mysticism to the ceremony, that you certainly don't get in the methodist chapel. Yes, it was pure ceremony yesterday morning . . . I experienced a strong feeling of uplift.'

Jackson eyed his sister-in-law speculatively.

'I'm glad you enjoyed it all May,' said Edith quickly, spotting the mischievous twinkle in her husband's eye.

'No, no,' Jackson explained. 'I don't mean that it makes that sort of sense.'

'What do you mean then?' questioned an irate May.

'I was thinking more about speaking a sensible language.'

'How can Latin be a sensible language?' asked a surprised Esther, 'after all, Latin is a dead language, surely English, French or Spanish would be a better choice if the Catholic church wants the whole world to understand their message?'

'Allow your father to explain what he means Esther . . . I'm sure he intends to say something sensible, don't you Jackson?'

'It's just a thought May, priests are no fools you know, they're very well educated, or so I'm told. To me it seems only common sense to speak a language that only the dead can understand . . . and a few of the living.'

'That's a silly thing to say Jackson, most Catholics can understand Latin, they learn it at school, it's special church

Latin,' explained Edith sharply, worried in case her husband was about to say something to shock her sister.

'Let him finish putting his point of view Edith, I'm sure he will make it clear shortly,' said a pointedly patient May.

'Not being blessed with the standard of education the rest of you have reached, puts me at a disadvantage, but it seems to me that there are a lot of advantages in mumbo-jumbo language, it's a bit like the witch doctors in Africa. Because it's so mysterious the congregation reckons there's a bit of magic working for them. No doubt you'll have noticed how priests and vicars keep their backs to you and expect you to shut your eyes! It's all to make you think they're performing some sort of miracle . . . they're afraid that if you get too close a look you might be able to manage one for yourself! That is . . . if you ask my opinion . . . and you did.'

'Heavens above!' laughed Esther, 'I've never heard a theological point of view to match that!'

'Is that what you call it?' hissed May in shocked disdain, '. . . for God's sake don't repeat such blasphemy in the hearing of the respectable churchgoers in our family . . . what would they think of our Edith married to a man with so little knowledge of the Church's teaching . . . even the natives in Africa know more of the scriptures than your poor Jackson, Edith.'

'Take no notice of him May, he's just a little confused by a service in a strange church. How about another cup of tea and a slice of this fruit cake I made earlier in the week? I've been waiting to cut into it when someone special came.'

Edith busied herself around the table in an attempt to divert attention from Jackson's supposed blasphemy . . . after all it was a serious matter, if May, who seemed to know about such things, felt that he held views unaccept-able to the established churches.

'And another thing . . .'

'Never mind 'another thing' Edith almost pleaded with

her husband, 'the wedding was lovely, I thought Claire was beautiful . . . and didn't you see those pretty bridesmaids May? A sight for sore eyes in their gorgeous pink dresses.'

'A pretty penny those would cost Edith. I'm glad you insisted on Jackson buying a new suit, all of Claire's family had spared no expense. I didn't see anything that looked as if it had been worn before.'

'Just as long as you two lasses don't expect me to buy a new suit for either of your weddings . . . this one'll have to do . . . it'll be black suits only from now on.'

'Why's that Dad?'

'Once you two are married there'll only be funerals to attend, so I can't see any sense in wasting good money on light-coloured suits like the one your mother persuaded me to buy last week. Clive Nicholson in the Co-op drapery department had a big enough shock when I called there last week to buy a fancy blue suit . . . said he couldn't remember ever measuring me for anything other than a pair of corduroy breeches.'

'What a cheek! You'd think we had no idea how to dress for a special occasion!'

'Yes Edith, you've allowed him to dress like a common roadman, no one would have been surprised at my George buying good suits, it was as much as could be expected . . . you've been much too lax about important matters Edith. I will avoid going into the Co-op in future . . .'

'I'm surprised you go into the Co-op at all May, but, come to think of it . . . you'll need your 'divvy' like everybody else.

'Indeed I don't! My savings stay in there year in and year out . . . if you want to know . . . it's there for my funeral . . . should a little extra be required.'

'What extra? Maybe you fancy some posh marble kerbs round your grave, like some wealthy Egremont families have. I reckon they're there to keep stray dogs and careless feet off their property . . . when they can't chase them off like they used to do when they were alive.'

'I hope I'll have a lovely wedding like Bill's,' sighed Esther changing the subject.

'Who has to pay for it?' asked Jackson guardedly.

'You, of course, the bride's father has to pay, I'm sure you know that Dad.'

'I thought I'd paid for the one yesterday.'

'No you didn't, we only paid for the cars and the flowers, that's traditional.'

'I was sure we'd paid for the lot, it cost me enough. I could have bought a couple of good milking cows with the cheque I signed.'

'I hope you think I'm worth more than a couple of milk cows, because I can tell you right now that it'll cost you a bit more than yesterday's cheque to get me married off. It always costs more to get rid of daughters!'

'She'll have to marry a Methodist Jackson and save you a bit of expense on the drinks,' said May tartly.

'A good idea May, I'm glad you thought of that, if I'd said anything, I'd have been accused of meanness . . . remember Esther, only Methodists will have your Aunt May's . . . and my approval.'

'As long as you choose a nice lad who'll be good to you I don't care which church door he darkens.'

'Thanks Mam, I know who's on my side. You needn't worry, I haven't met anyone I fancy yet. The lads round here aren't worth a second glance. Your money's safe for a bit yet Dad.'

'Thank God for that,' said a satisfied Jackson.

'I forgot to mention earlier that I noticed your lovely tea-set Edith, did you buy it especially for Bill's wedding?'

'No May, I bought it in a sale a good many years ago . . . just on spec as you might say. I knew there'd be a special occasion one day when I could display it. I bought it in a house sale, it had belonged to a wealthy family who had probably never used it.'

'Yes, it's real quality china, just look at this cup.' May held the cup up to the light to show its translucence.

'Where on earth have you kept these lovely things hidden? I've never seen it on display on your dresser.'

'No, I put it away safely at the back of a cupboard, I was afraid it might get damaged on display.'

'Yes May,' interrupted Jackson happily, 'good china is like a good woman . . . the best bits are hidden from view!'
May rose to her feet, earrings swirling in total disharmony. 'I won't stay here another minute and listen to such coarse speech . . . my coat Esther please, it's time to walk to catch my bus anyway . . '

Esther, her shoulders heaving with repressed laughter, hastened to do her aunt's bidding.

'I'll walk that far with you,' volunteered a flustered Edith.

'And I'll get started on my beasts, they must think I've gone to another wedding the way they've been neglected today.'

Then as he reached for his cap and stick he muttered, half to himself, and half to a chuckling Esther . . .

'. . . hypocritical old windbag!'